Ten Adorab
Teddy Bea

Ten Adorable Teddy Bears to Knit

plus all their clothes and accessories

Rachel Borello

BARRON'S

A QUARTO BOOK

First edition for the United States
and Canada published in 2015 by
Barron's Educational Series, Inc.

All inquiries should be
addressed to:
Barron's Educational Series, Inc.
250 Wireless Boulevard
Hauppauge, NY 11788
www.barronseduc.com

ISBN: 978-1-4380-0656-7
Library of Congress Control No:
2015931284

Conceived, designed, and
produced by
Quarto Publishing plc
The Old Brewery
6 Blundell Street
London N7 9BH

QUAR.TBKN

Project editor: Chelsea Edwards
Photographer: Simon Pask
Illustrator: Victoria Woodgate
Design assistant: Martina Calvio
Proofreader: Sarah Hoggett
Pattern checker: Ashley Knowlton
Indexer: Helen Snaith
Art director: Caroline Guest
Creative director: Moira Clinch
Publisher: Paul Carslake

Color separation in Singapore by
Pica Digital Pte Limited
Printed in China by Toppan
Leefung Pte Limited

10 9 8 7 6 5 4 3 2 1

Contents

Bear patterns   8

Accessory patterns   68

Bear necessities   92

Welcome to my knitting world!

When I was young, my mom taught me to crochet. I made miniature blankets for my cats. When I got to college, my roommate knew how to knit, and we were fascinated with each other's skills. She gave me knitting lessons, and I taught her crochet. I was immediately entranced by the knitted fabric and the possibility of a wide range of garments that were not only wearable, but possibly even fashionable! A few years of unfinished sweaters and afghans taught me that large projects were possibly not my forte. Around that time, crocheted toys were sprouting up all over the Internet. I thought if toys could be made out of knitting instead of crochet, the possibility existed for smoother lines, more distinct shapes, and beautiful colorwork. The first toy I designed was a tiny teddy bear, who I gave to my nephew when he was born. In the years since, I have honed my craft, but I always find myself coming back to teddy bears. There's something about a teddy bear that's so universally well loved that they just make perfect projects. I hope you enjoy knitting these teddy bears as much as I enjoyed designing them, and that you come away from this book with a renewed sense of amazement at the beautiful profiles and characters you can create with two sticks and a bit of string.

Rachel Borello

About this book

In this delightful new book, you will discover how to knit gorgeous teddy bears along with unique accessories to dress them in. There are 10 bear patterns for you to select from, and insightful tips and techniques to help you assemble your chosen bear.

Chapter 1: Bear and accessory patterns, pages 8–91

At the heart of this book are 10 enchanting bear patterns. Each unique pattern features full written instructions, beautiful photographs, and guidance on all the tools and materials you will need to bring your bear to life. Also included in this section are the adorable accessory patterns for you to pair with your bear.

Chapter 2: Bear necessities, pages 92–107

These pages feature everything you need to know to get started, from a summary of all the tools and materials you will need to detailed instructions on core techniques. An illustrated, comprehensive, and concise guide helps you to work the basic knitting stitches, evenly stuff your bear, and embroider characterful faces.

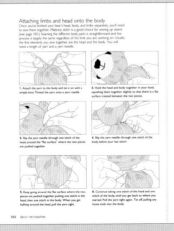

Bea

Bea is a beautiful, classic-style teddy. She knits up so quickly and easily in worsted-weight yarn, you will want to make one in every color. Everyone who sees her is going to want a Bea for themselves.

Winter hat, see page 72

You will need:

- Set of five US size 5 (3.75 mm) double-pointed knitting needles (dpns)
- 50 yd (46 m) of worsted-weight yarn
- Contrast color yarn for snout
- Small amount of black worsted-weight yarn for embroidering nose
- 1 set of ½ in (12 mm) black acrylic safety eyes
- Small amount of black embroidery floss for embroidering mouth
- Polyester fiberfill stuffing
- Yarn needle
- Scissors

Cardigan, see page 73

Pinafore, see page 76

BEAR'S HEIGHT

10 in
(25.5 cm)

Gauge

12 sts by 14 rows = 2 in (5 cm) square in stockinette stitch

Instructions

HEAD:

Cast on 6 sts in snout color.

Round 1: [Kfb] 6 times, distribute sts evenly over 4 dpns, and join to work in the round. (12 sts)

Round 2: [Kfb, k4, kfb] twice. (16 sts)

Round 3: [Kfb, k2, kfb, k4] twice. (20 sts)

Round 4: [Kfb, k4, kfb, k4] twice. (24 sts)

Rounds 5–7: K all sts.

Round 8: P all sts.

Cut snout color and join main color.

Round 9: K11, [kfb] twice, k1, kfb, k2, kfb, k1, [kfb] twice, k3. (30 sts)

Round 10: K14, kfb, k1, kfb, k4, kfb, k1, kfb, k6. (34 sts)

Round 11: K12, [kfb] twice, k4, kfb, k4, kfb, k4, [kfb] twice, k4. (40 sts)

Round 12: K all sts.

Round 13: K14, kfb, k18, kfb, k6. (42 sts)

Round 14: K15, kfb, k18, kfb, k7. (44 sts)

Round 15: K16, kfb, k18, kfb, k8. (46 sts)

Round 16: K17, kfb, k18, kfb, k9. (48 sts)

Round 17: K18, kfb, k18, kfb, k10. (50 sts)

Rounds 18–33: K all sts.

Embroider on nose and attach eyes. Stuff head, being sure to add extra stuffing to snout.

Round 34: K18, [k2tog] twice, k14, [k2tog] twice, k8. (46 sts)

Round 35: K17, [k2tog] twice, k12, [k2tog] twice, k7. (42 sts)

Round 36: K16, [k2tog] twice, k8, [k2tog] twice, k6. (38 sts)

Round 37: [K2tog] 19 times. (19 sts)

Round 38: [K2tog] 9 times, k1. (10 sts)

Cut yarn, leaving a long tail, and thread onto a yarn needle. Thread yarn through remaining live sts, pull tight, and tie off.

EARS (make 2):

Cast on 3 sts.

Round 1: [Kfb] 3 times, distribute sts evenly over 2 dpns, and join to work in the round. (6 sts total)

Round 2: [Kfb, k1, kfb] twice. (10 sts)

Round 3: [Kfb, k3, kfb] twice. (14 sts)

Rounds 4–7: K all sts.

Bind off all sts and flatten out ear. Sew to side of head.

BODY:

Cast on 3 sts.

Round 1: [Kfb] 3 times. (6 sts)

Round 2: [Kfb] 6 times. (12 sts)

Round 3: [K1, kfb] 6 times. (18 sts)

Round 4: [K2, kfb] 6 times. (24 sts)

Round 5: [K3, kfb] 6 times. (30 sts)

Round 6: [K4, kfb] 6 times. (36 sts)

Round 7: [K5, kfb] 6 times. (42 sts)

Rounds 8–12: K all sts.

Round 13: K14, [k2, k2tog] 3 times, k16. (39 sts)

Round 14: K14, [k1, k2tog] 3 times, k16. (36 sts)

Rounds 15–18: K all sts.

Round 19: K2, k2tog, [k8, k2tog] 3 times, k2. (32 sts)

Round 20: K all sts.

Round 21: K2, k2tog, k6, k2tog, k8, k2tog, k6, k2tog, k2. (28 sts)

Continue to decrease at shoulder until decreases come together.

K 2 rounds.

K2tog all sts.

Stuff. Cut yarn, leaving a long tail, thread yarn through remaining live sts, pull tight, and tie off. Sew to head.

ARMS (make 2):

Cast on 3 sts.

Round 1: [Kfb] 3 times, distribute sts evenly over 2 dpns, and join to work in the round. (6 sts)

Round 2: [Kfb, k1, kfb] twice. (10 sts)

Round 3: [Kfb, k3, kfb] twice. (14 sts)

Rounds 4–10: K all sts.

Round 11: K2tog, k4, [kfb] twice, k4, k2tog. (14 sts)

Rounds 12–15: K all sts.

Round 16: K2tog, k10, k2tog. (12 sts)

Rounds 17–18: K all sts.

Round 19: K2tog, k8, k2tog. (10 sts)

Round 20: K all sts.

Round 21: K2tog, k6, k2tog. (8 sts)

Round 22: K all sts.

Stuff arm.

Round 23: K2tog, k4, k2tog. (6 sts)

Rounds 24 & 25: K all sts

Cut yarn, leaving a long tail and thread onto a yarn needle. Thread yarn through remaining live sts, pull tight, and tie off. Sew to shoulder.

LEGS (make 2):

Cast on 3 sts.

Round 1: [Kfb] 3 times, distribute sts evenly over 3 dpns, and join to work in the round. (6 sts)

Round 2: [Kfb] 6 times. (12 sts)

Round 3: [K1, kfb] 6 times. (18 sts)

Round 4: [K5, kfb] 3 times. (21 sts)

Rounds 5–8: K all sts.

Round 9: K6, [k2tog] 5 times, k5. (16 sts)

Round 10: K6, [k2tog] 3 times, k4. (13 sts)

Rounds 11–26: K all sts.

Bind off all sts. Stuff foot and leg, and sew to body.

Finishing

Secure any remaining ends inside body. Wash gently and let dry.

Junior

Junior is Bea's little brother bear. They make a great pair when knitted together, and Junior's small stature makes him a quick project.

Beanie, see page 72

You will need:

- Set of five US size 3 (3.25 mm) double-pointed knitting needles (dpns)
- 50 yd (46 m) of worsted-weight yarn
- Small amount of worsted-weight yarn in slightly different color for snout
- Small amount of black worsted-weight yarn for embroidering nose
- 1 set of ½ in (12 mm) black acrylic safety eyes
- Small amount of dark brown embroidery floss for embroidering mouth
- Polyester fiberfill stuffing
- Yarn needle

Backpack, see page 68

Sleeping bag, see page 80

BEAR'S HEIGHT

7 in
(17.5 cm)

Gauge

12 sts by 14 rows = 2 in (5 cm) square in stockinette stitch

Instructions

HEAD:

With yarn in snout color, cast on 6 sts.

Round 1: [Kfb] 6 times. Distribute sts evenly over 4 dpns and join to work in the round. (12 sts)

Round 2: [Kfb, k4, kfb] twice. (16 sts)

Round 3: [Kfb, k2, kfb, k4] twice. (20 sts)

Round 4: [Kfb, k4, kfb, k4] twice. (24 sts)

Rounds 5–6: K all sts.

Round 7: P all sts.

Cut snout color and join main yarn.

Round 8: K11, [kfb] twice, k1, kfb, k2, kfb, k1, [kfb] twice, k3. (30 sts)

Round 9: K14, kfb, k1, kfb, k4, kfb, k1, kfb, k6. (34 sts)

Round 10: K12, [kfb] twice, [k4, kfb] twice, k4, [kfb] twice, k4. (40 sts)

Round 11: K all sts.

Round 12: K14, kfb, k18, kfb, k6. (42 sts)

Round 13: K15, kfb, k18, kfb, k7. (44 sts)

Round 14: K16, kfb, k18, kfb, k8. (46 sts)

Rounds 15–26: K all sts.

Embroider nose and mouth and attach eyes, referring to photo for guidance. Stuff head firmly, making sure to add extra stuffing to snout.

Round 27: K16, [k2tog] twice, k14, [k2tog] twice, k8. (42 sts)

Round 28: K15, [k2tog] twice, k12, [k2tog] twice, k7. (38 sts)

Round 29: K14, [k2tog] twice, k10, [k2tog] twice, k6. (34 sts)

Round 30: [K2tog] 17 times. (17 sts)

Round 31: [K2tog] 8 times, k1. (9 sts)

Add any more stuffing as needed, cut yarn, and thread onto a yarn needle. Thread yarn through remaining live sts, pull tight, and tie off.

EARS (make 2):

With main yarn, cast on 3 sts.

Round 1: [Kfb] 3 times. Distribute sts evenly over 2 dpns and join to work in the round. (6 sts)

Round 2: [Kfb, k1, kfb] twice. (10 sts)

Round 3: [Kfb, k3, kfb] twice. (14 sts)

Rounds 4–6: K all sts.

Bind off all sts and flatten ear. Sew to side of head.

BODY:

With main yarn, cast on 3 sts.

Round 1: [Kfb] 3 times. Distribute sts evenly over 3 dpns and join to work in the round. (6 sts)

Round 2: [Kfb] 6 times. (12 sts)

Round 3: [K1, kfb] 6 times. (18 sts)

Round 4: [K2, kfb] 6 times. (24 sts)

Round 5: [K3, kfb] 6 times. (30 sts)

Round 6: [K4, kfb] 6 times. (36 sts)

Rounds 7–9: K all sts.

Round 10: K12, [k2, k2tog] 3 times, k12. (33 sts)

Round 11: K12, [k1, k2tog] 3 times, k12. (30 sts)

Rounds 12–13: K all sts.

Round 14: K2, [k2tog, k6] 3 times, k2tog, k2. (26 sts)

Round 15: K2, k2tog, k4, k2tog, k6, k2tog, k4, k2tog, k2. (22 sts)

Round 16: [K2, k2tog] twice, [k2tog, k2] twice. (18 sts)

Round 17: [K2tog] 9 times. (9 sts)

Stuff body firmly. Cut yarn, leaving a long tail, and thread onto a yarn needle. Thread yarn through remaining live sts, pull tight, and tie off. Decreases in Rounds 10–11 form the top of the potbelly. Decreases in Rounds 14–16 form the shoulders at the sides. Use these as guides to align the belly as the front of the body and sew to head accordingly.

ARMS (make 2):
With main yarn, cast on 3 sts.
Round 1: [Kfb] 3 times. Distribute sts evenly over 2 dpns and join to work in the round. (6 sts)
Round 2: [Kfb, k1, kfb] twice. (10 sts)
Rounds 3–8: K all sts.
Round 9: K2tog, k2, [kfb] twice, k2, k2tog. (10 sts)
Rounds 10–12: K all sts.
Round 13: K2tog, k6, k2tog. (8 sts)

Stuff the arm.

Round 14: K2tog, k4, k2tog. (6 sts)
Round 15: K2tog, k2, k2tog. (4 sts)
Cut yarn, leaving a long tail, and thread onto a yarn needle. Thread yarn through remaining sts, pull tight, and tie off. Roll the arm lightly between your hands to distribute the stuffing evenly throughout and obtain the correct shape. Sew to shoulder of body, with the k2tog decreases from Rounds 13–15 on the outside of the arm—they form the gentle slope of the outer shoulder.

LEGS (make 2):
With main yarn, cast on 3 sts.
Round 1: [Kfb] 3 times. Distribute sts evenly over 3 dpns and join to work in the round. (6 sts)

Round 2: [Kfb] 6 times. (12 sts)
Round 3: [K3, kfb] 3 times. (15 sts)
Rounds 4–6: K all sts.
Round 7: K5, [k2tog] 3 times, k4. (12 sts)
Rounds 8–16: K all sts.
Bind off all sts. Stuff foot and leg firmly and sew to body, being sure to face the "foot" (formed by the decreases in Round 7) forward.

Finishing
Secure any remaining ends inside body. Wash gently and let dry.

Clarke

Clarke is here to save the day with his super fluffiness! He's knitted from a slightly fuzzy alpaca yarn, and a runover with a wire-bristled brush gives him his long-furred appearance.

You will need:

- Pair of US size 3 (3.25 mm) knitting needles
- 130 yd (120 m) of worsted-weight alpaca blend yarn
- Small amount of brown embroidery floss for embroidering mouth
- Small amount of brown worsted-weight yarn for embroidering nose
- 1 set of ½ in (12 mm) acrylic safety eyes
- Polyester fiberfill stuffing
- Slicker brush or similar wire-bristled brush
- Yarn needle

Superhero mask, see page 88

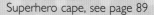

Superhero cape, see page 89

Shorts, see page 84

BEAR'S HEIGHT

9 in
(23 cm)

Gauge

10 sts by 14 rows = 2 in (5 cm) square in stockinette stitch

Special stitch

Kfbf: Knit through front loop, then back loop, then front loop again to increase by two

Note

When using a yarn with loft in a tight gauge, most of the "fur" of the yarn will be trapped in the stitches, instead of forming a halo of fur. By brushing it in all directions with a wire brush, you can pull all the fibers to the outside and give your teddy bear a great look.

Instructions

HEAD:

Cast on 6 sts.
Row 1 (RS): K all sts.
Row 2 and all even (WS) rows: P all sts.
Row 3: [K2, M1] twice, k2. (8 sts)
Row 5: [K2, kfbf] twice, k2. (12 sts)
Row 7: K4, kfbf, k2, kfbf, k4. (16 sts)
Row 9: K3, [kfbf] twice, k6, [kfbf] twice, k3. (24 sts)
Row 11: Kfb, k4, [kfbf] twice, k10, [kfbf] twice, k4, kfb. (34 sts)
Row 13: Kfb, k7, [kfbf] twice, k14, [kfbf] twice, k7, kfb. (44 sts)
Row 15: K12, [kfb, k2] 3 times, kfb, [kfb, k2] 3 times, kfb, k12. (52 sts)
Row 17: K12, [kfb, k3] 3 times, kfb, k2, [kfb, k3] 3 times, kfb, k12. (60 sts)
Rows 19–32: Work in st st.
Row 33: [K2tog] 30 times. (30 sts)
Row 35: [K2tog] 15 times. (15 sts)

Row 36 (WS): P all sts.
Cut yarn, leaving a long tail, and thread onto a yarn needle. Thread yarn through remaining live sts, pull tight, and tie off. This forms the back of the head. Brush out the piece. Attach eyes and embroider on nose and mouth, using photo for guidance. Sew the head together with a seam that stretches down from the back of the head, under the neck region, then back up under the nose; when there is approximately a 1-in (3-cm) opening left, stuff the head firmly. After stuffing and seaming have been completed, you may want to go over the head again with the brush to do some final adjustments.

EARS (make 2):

Cast on 6 sts.
Row 1 and all odd (RS) rows: K all sts.
Row 2 (WS): [Kfb] 6 times. (12 sts)
Row 4: [K1, Kfb] 6 times. (18 sts)
Row 6: [K2, Kfb] 6 times. (24 sts)
Rows 7–10: Starting with a RS row, work in st st. Bind off and brush out. Fold ear in half widthwise and sew side seam, then sew cast-on edge to head.

BODY:

Cast on 20 sts.
Rows 1–4: Starting with a RS row, work in st st.
Row 5 (RS): K5, M1, k10, M1, k5. (22 sts)
Row 6 and every foll even (WS) row: P all sts.
Row 7: K5, kfb, k10, kfb, k5. (24 sts)
Row 9: K6, M1, k12, M1, k6. (26 sts)
Row 11: K6, kfb, k12, kfb, k6. (28 sts)
Row 13: K7, M1, k14, M1, k7. (30 sts)
Row 15: K7, kfb, k14, kfb, k7. (32 sts)
Row 17: K8, M1, k16, M1, k8. (34 sts)

Row 19: K8, kfb, k16, kfb, k8. (36 sts)

Rows 21–26: Work in st st.

Row 27: [K2tog] 18 times. (18 sts)

Row 29: [K2tog] 9 times. (9 sts)

Row 30 (WS): P all sts.

Cut yarn, leaving a long tail, and thread onto a yarn needle. Thread yarn through remaining live sts, pull tight, and tie off. Brush out body. Sew seam up back of body, stuff, and sew cast-on edge to bottom of head.

ARMS (make 2):

Cast on 16 sts.

Rows 1–18: Starting with a RS row, work in st st.

Row 19 (RS): [K2tog] 8 times. (8 sts)

Cut yarn, leaving a long tail, and thread onto a yarn needle. Thread yarn through remaining live sts, pull tight, and tie off. Brush out. Fold arm in half lengthwise and sew up back of arm. Stuff arm, then sew cast-on edge to shoulder.

LEGS (make 2):

Cast on 20 sts.

Rows 1–20: Starting with a RS row, work in st st.

Row 21 (RS): [K2tog] 10 times. (10 sts)

Cut yarn, leaving a long tail, and thread onto a yarn needle. Thread yarn through remaining live sts, pull tight, and tie off. Brush out. Fold leg in half lengthwise and sew up back of leg. Stuff leg, then sew cast-on edge to bottom of body.

Finishing

Secure any remaining ends inside body. Wash gently and let dry. Brush out once more, if desired.

Peta

Peta's button eyes and joints give her a wonderful, classic teddy-bear look. If you don't want to do the joints, or are making her for a very small child, she would work just as well with her limbs simply sewn on.

You will need:

- Set of four US size 3 (3.25 mm) double-pointed knitting needles (dpns)
- 220 yd (200 m) of worsted-weight yarn
- Two ½ in (12 mm) black buttons for eyes
- Four small tan buttons for joints
- Small amount of black worsted-weight yarn for embroidering nose and mouth
- Polyester fiberfill stuffing
- Tapestry thread and long sewing needle
- Yarn needle

Winter hat, see page 72

Fringed scarf, see page 75

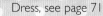

Dress, see page 71

BEAR'S HEIGHT

10 in
(25.5 cm)

Gauge

11 sts by 15 rows = 2 in (5 cm) square in stockinette stitch

Special stitch

Kfbf: Knit through front loop, then back loop, then front loop again to increase by two

Note

Body is very narrow at the top and bottom because of the way the arms and legs are attached. It will end up being almost diamond-shaped.

Instructions

HEAD:

Cast on 6 sts.

Set-up round: K all sts. Distribute sts evenly over 3 dpns and join to work in the round.

Round 1: K1, kfbf, k1, kfbf, k2. (10 sts)

Round 2 and every foll even round through Round 12: K all sts.

Round 3: K2, kfbf, k3, kfbf, k3. (14 sts)

Round 5: K3, kfbf, k5, kfbf, k4. (18 sts)

Round 7: K4, kfbf, k7, kfbf, k5. (22 sts)

Round 9: K6, kfbf, k7, kfbf, k7. (26 sts)

Round 11: K7, kfbf, k9, kfbf, k8. (30 sts)

Round 13: K9, kfbf, k9, kfbf, k10. (34 sts)

Round 14 (even round): K11, kfbf, k9, kfbf, k12. (38 sts)

Round 15: K13, kfbf, k9, kfbf, k14. (42 sts)

Round 16: K15, kfbf, k9, kfbf, k16. (46 sts)

Round 17: K17, kfbf, k9, kfbf, k18. (50 sts)

Round 18: K19, kfbf, k9, kfbf, k20. (54 sts)

Round 19: K21, kfbf, k9, kfbf, k22. (58 sts)

Round 20: K23, kfbf, k9, kfbf, k24. (62 sts)

Rounds 21–34: K all sts.

Round 35: K24, k2tog, k9, k2tog, k25. (60 sts)

Round 36: K23, k2tog, k9, k2tog, k24. (58 sts)

Round 37: K22, k2tog, k9, k2tog, k23. (56 sts)

Round 38: K21, k2tog, k9, k2tog, k22. (54 sts)

Round 39: K20, k2tog, k9, k2tog, k21. (52 sts)

Round 40: K19, k2tog, k9, k2tog, k20. (50 sts)

Round 41: [K2tog] 25 times. (25 sts)

Stuff head firmly, pushing extra stuffing into snout.

Round 42: [K2tog] 12 times, k1. (13 sts)

Finish stuffing head. Cut yarn, leaving a long tail, and thread onto a yarn needle. Thread yarn through remaining live sts, pull tight, and tie off. Embroider on nose and mouth and sew on button eyes, referring to photo for guidance.

EARS (make 2):

Cast on 24 sts. Distribute sts evenly over 2 dpns and join to work in the round.

Rounds 1–6: K all sts.

Round 7: [K2tog, k8, k2tog] twice. (20 sts)

Round 8: [K2tog, k6, k2tog] twice. (16 sts)

Round 9: [K2tog, k4, k2tog] twice. (12 sts)

Round 10: [K2tog, k2, k2tog] twice. (8 sts)

Round 11: [K2tog] 4 times. (4 sts)

Cut yarn, leaving a long tail, and thread onto a yarn needle. Thread yarn through remaining live sts, pull tight, and tie off. Sew cast-on edge of ear to head.

BODY:

Cast on 6 sts.

Set-up round: K all sts. Distribute sts evenly over 3 dpns and join to work in the round.

Round 1: K1, kfbf, k2, kfbf, k1. (10 sts)

Round 2: K2, kfbf, k4, kfbf, k2. (14 sts)

Round 3: K3, kfbf, k6, kfbf, k3. (18 sts)

Rounds 4, 6, and 8: K all sts.

Round 5: K4, kfbf, k8, kfbf, k4. (22 sts)

Round 7: K5, kfbf, k10, kfbf, k5. (26 sts)
Round 9: K6, kfbf, k12, kfbf, k6. (30 sts)
Round 10: K7, kfbf, k14, kfbf, k7. (34 sts)
Round 11: K8, kfbf, k16, kfbf, k8. (38 sts)
Round 12: K9, kfbf, k18, kfbf, k9. (42 sts)
Rounds 13–22: K all sts.
Round 23: [K2tog] twice, k5, sk2p, k5, [k2tog] 4 times, k5, sk2p, k5, [k2tog] twice. (30 sts)
Round 24: [K2tog] twice, k1, sk2p, k3, [k2tog] 4 times, k3, sk2p, k1, [k2tog] twice. (18 sts)
Stuff body firmly.
Round 25: K2, [k2tog] twice, k6, [k2tog] twice, k2. (14 sts)
Round 26: K3, k2tog, k4, k2tog, k3. (12 sts)
Rounds 27–30: K all sts.
Finish stuffing body. Cut yarn, leaving a long tail, and thread onto a yarn needle. Thread yarn through remaining live sts, pull tight, and tie off. Cast-on edge is bottom of body, and Round 30 is at neck. Sew neck to bottom of head. Secure ends inside body.

ARMS (make 2):
Cast on 6 sts.
Round 1: [Kfb] 6 times. Distribute sts evenly over 3 dpns and join to work in the round. (12 sts)
Round 2: K all sts.
Round 3: [K1, kfb] 6 times. (18 sts)
Rounds 4–19: K all sts.
Rounds 20–26: K2tog, knit to end.
11 sts remain after Round 26 has been completed. Stuff arm. Cut yarn, leaving a long tail, and thread onto a yarn needle. Thread yarn through remaining live sts, pull tight and tie off.

LEGS (make 2):
Cast on 6 sts.

Round 1: [Kfb] 6 times. Distribute sts evenly over 3 dpns and join to work in the round. (12 sts)
Round 2: K all sts.
Round 3: [K1, kfb] 6 times. (18 sts)
Round 4: K all sts.
Round 5: [K2, kfb] 6 times. (24 sts)
Rounds 6–15: K all sts.
Rounds 16–28: K2tog, knit to end.
11 sts remain after Round 28 has been completed. Stuff leg. Cut yarn, leaving a long tail, and thread onto a yarn needle. Thread yarn through remaining live sts, pull tight, and tie off.

Finishing

Sew cast-on edge of body to head. Position narrow ends of arms and legs against body to prepare for sewing on. See page 103 for instructions on how to make Peta's limbs jointed.

Secure any remaining ends inside body. Wash gently and let dry.

Emmeline

Emmeline has intricate cableknit detail on her head and body. The cables are very simple and can be done with or without a cable needle, so they are great for someone who is new to cablework.

Beret, see page 78

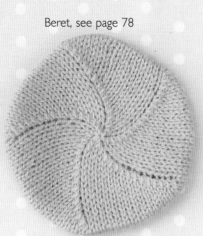

You will need:

- Set of five US size 3 (3.25 mm) double-pointed knitting needles (dpns)
- 120 yd (110 m) of sport-weight yarn
- Cable needle
- Small amount of black worsted-weight yarn for embroidering nose
- 1 set of ½ in (12 mm) black acrylic safety eyes
- Small amount of dark brown embroidery floss for embroidering mouth
- Polyester fiberfill stuffing
- Yarn needle

Fringed scarf, see page 75

Backpack, see page 68

BEAR'S HEIGHT

10 in
(25.5 cm)

Gauge

12 sts by 14 rows = 2 in (5 cm) square in stockinette stitch

Special stitch

C4B: Cable 4 back. Slip next 2 sts onto a cable needle, hold to the back, knit the next 2 sts, then knit the sts off the cable needle.

Instructions

HEAD:

Cast on 3 sts.
Round 1: [Kfb] 3 times. Distribute sts evenly over 3 dpns and join to work in the round. (6 sts)
Round 2: [Kfb] 6 times. (12 sts)
Round 3: [K1, kfb] 6 times. (18 sts)
Round 4: [K2, kfb] 6 times. (24 sts)
Round 5: K all sts.
Round 6: [K3, kfb] 6 times. (30 sts)
Rounds 7–8: K all sts.
Round 9: P all sts.
Round 10: K10, [kfb] 8 times, p4, [kfb] 8 times. (46 sts)
Rounds 11–14: K10, [p4, k4] 4 times, p4.
Round 15: K10, [p4, C4B] 4 times, p4.
Repeat Rounds 11–15 three times more.

The panel of 10 knitted stitches is the bottom of the head; the eyes should be attached just below the two uppermost cables. Embroider nose and mouth and attach eyes. Stuff the head firmly.

Round 31: K10, [p2tog twice, k4] 4 times, [p2tog] twice. (36 sts)
Round 32: [K2tog] 5 times, [p2tog, k4] 4 times, p2tog. (26 sts)

Round 33: K5, [p1, k2tog twice] 4 times, p1 (18 sts)
Round 34: [K2tog] 9 times. (9 sts)

Add any more stuffing as needed, cut yarn and thread onto a yarn needle. Thread yarn through remaining live sts, pull tight, and tie off, securing end on inside of head.

EARS (make 2):

Cast on 7 sts.
Rows 1–7: K all sts.
Row 8: K1, k2tog, k1, k2tog, k1. (5 sts)
Row 9: K all sts.
Row 10: K1, sk2p, k1. (3 sts)
Row 11: Sk2p. (1 st)
Cut yarn, leaving a long tail, and thread onto a yarn needle. Thread yarn through remaining live st. Pull tight and, using your yarn needle, weave the end straight down from the top of the ear to the base. This will help you to round out the top of your ear. When you are satisfied with the shape of the ear, tie off end and sew cast-on edge of ear to side of head.

BODY:

Cast on 6 sts.
Round 1: [Kfb] 6 times. Distribute sts evenly over 3 dpns and join to work in the round. (12 sts)
Round 2: [Kfb, k2, kfb] 3 times. (18 sts)
Round 3: [Kfb, p4, kfb] 3 times. (24 sts)
Round 4: [Kfb, k1, p4, k1, kfb] 3 times. (30 sts)
Round 5: [Kfb, k2, p4, k2, kfb] 3 times. (36 sts)
Round 6: [Kfb, k3, p4, k3, kfb] 3 times. (42 sts)
Round 7: [Kfb, k4, p4, k4, kfb] 3 times. (48 sts)
Round 8: [P2, k4, p4, k4, p2] 3 times.
Round 9: [P2, C4B, p2, M1, p2, C4B, p2] 3 times. (51 sts)

Rounds 10–13: [P2, k4, p2, k1, p2, k4, p2] 3 times.

Round 14: [P2, C4B, p2, k1, p2, C4B, p2] 3 times.

Repeat Rounds 10–14 twice more.

Round 25: [P2tog, k4, p2tog, k1, p2tog, k4, p2tog] 3 times. (39 sts)

Round 26: [P1, k4, p1, k1, p1, k4, p1] 3 times.

Round 27: [P1, k4, p3tog, k4, p1] 3 times. (33 sts)

Round 28: [P1, k4, p1, k4, p1] 3 times.

Round 29: [P1, C4B, p1, C4B, p1] 3 times.

Round 30: [P1, k2tog twice, p1, k2tog twice, p1] 3 times. (21 sts)

Round 31: [P1, k2, p1, k2, p1] 3 times. Stuff body, being careful not to stretch out the fabric.

Round 32: [K2tog, sk2p, k2tog] 3 times. (9 sts) Cut yarn, leaving a long tail, and thread onto a yarn needle. Thread yarn through remaining live sts, pull tight, and tie off.

LEGS (make 2):
Cast on 6 sts.

Round 1: [Kfb] 6 times. Distribute sts evenly over 3 dpns and join to work in the round. (12 sts)

Round 2: [K1, kfb] 6 times. (18 sts)

Round 3: [K2, kfb] 6 times. (24 sts)

Rounds 4–8: K all sts.

Round 9: K8, [k2tog] 4 times, k8. (20 sts)

Rounds 10–13: K all sts.

Round 14: K2tog, k16, k2tog. (18 sts)

Rounds 15–17: K all sts.

Round 18: K2tog, k14, k2tog. (16 sts)

Rounds 19–34: K all sts.

Round 35: [K2tog] 8 times. (8 sts) Stuff leg. Cut yarn, leaving a long tail, and thread

onto a yarn needle. Thread yarn through remaining live sts, pull tight, and tie off. Sew to body at Round 35, being sure to face the "foot" (formed by the decreases in Round 9) forward.

ARMS (make 2):
Cast on 6 sts.

Round 1: [Kfb] 6 times. Distribute sts evenly over 3 dpns and join to work in the round. (12 sts)

Round 2: [K1, kfb] 6 times. (18 sts)

Rounds 3–16: K all sts.

Round 17: K2tog, knit to end of round. (1 st decreased)

Round 18: K all sts.

Repeat Rounds 17–18 five times more. (12 sts) Stuff arm.

Round 29: [K2tog] 6 times. (6 sts) Cut yarn, leaving a long tail, and thread onto a yarn needle. Thread yarn through remaining sts, pull tight, and tie off. Sew to body at shoulder, with decreases in Rounds 17–28 at the underside of the arm. Repeat for other side.

Finishing

Secure any remaining ends inside body. Wash gently and let dry.

Riley

Riley only has a small amount of stranded colorwork on her face to give her that iconic panda look, but it has a huge impact. She's knitted flat on two needles in a tight gauge in classic panda white and black.

You will need:

- Pair of US size 3 (3.25 mm) knitting needles
- 100 yd (92 m) of worsted-weight yarn in cream/natural (color A)
- 70 yd (64 m) of worsted-weight yarn in black (color B)
- 1 set of ½ in (12 mm) black acrylic safety eyes
- Small amount of black embroidery floss for embroidering mouth
- Polyester fiberfill stuffing
- Yarn needle

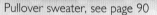

Pullover sweater, see page 90

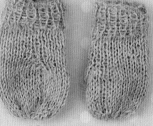

Shorts, see page 84

Socks, see page 87

BEAR'S HEIGHT

10 in
(25.5 cm)

Gauge

10 sts by 14 rows = 2 in (5 cm) square in stockinette stitch

Special stitch

Pfb: Purl through both the front and back loop to increase by one on the wrong side

Instructions

HEAD:

Cast on 6 sts with A.

Row 1 (RS): [Kfb] 6 times. (12 sts)

Row 2 (WS): P2, [pfb] twice, p4, [pfb] twice, p2. (16 sts)

Row 3: [K2, kfb] twice, k4, [kfb, k2] twice. (20 sts)

Row 4: P2, pfb, [p4, pfb] 3 times, p2. (24 sts)

Rows 5–8: Work in st st.

Join B and continue as follows:

Row 9 (RS): K4 in A, k3 in B, [kfb] twice in B, k1 in B, kfb in A, k2 in A, kfb in A, k1 in B, [kfb] twice in B, k3 in B, k4 in A. (30 sts)

Row 10: P4 in A, p6 in B, pfb in B, p1 in B, pfb in A, p4 in A, pfb in A, p1 in B, pfb in B, p6 in B, p4 in A. (34 sts)

Row 11: K5 in A, k3 in B, [kfb] twice in B, k2 in B, k2 in A, kfb in A, k4 in A, kfb in A, k2 in A, k2 in B, [kfb] twice in B, k3 in B, k5 in A. (40 sts)
Cut B and secure on WS.

Row 12 (WS): P all sts.

Row 13: K10, kfb, k18, kfb, k10. (42 sts)

Row 14: P11, pfb, p18, pfb, p11. (44 sts)

Row 15: K12, kfb, k18, kfb, k12. (46 sts)

Row 16: P13, pfb, p18, pfb, p13. (48 sts)

Row 17: K14, kfb, k18, kfb, k14. (50 sts)

Rows 18–33: Work in st st.

Row 34 (WS): P14, [p2tog] twice, p14, [p2tog] twice, p14. (46 sts)

Row 35: K13, [k2tog] twice, k12, [k2tog] twice, k13. (42 sts)

Row 36: P12, [p2tog] twice, p10, [p2tog] twice, p12. (38 sts)

Row 37: [K2tog] 19 times. (19 sts)

Row 38: P all sts.

Row 39: [K2tog] 9 times, k1. (10 sts)

Cut yarn, leaving a long tail, and thread onto a yarn needle. Thread yarn through remaining live sts, pull tight, and tie off. Row 39 is at the back of the head, and the cast-on edge is the tip of the nose. Sew the head together with a seam that stretches down from the back of the head, under the neck region, then back up under the nose. Be sure to stuff the head and attach eyes before the seam is finished. When the head is stuffed and sewn shut, embroider on nose and mouth, using photo for guidance. Pull any loose ends into the head to conceal.

EARS (make 2):

Cast on 3 sts with B.

Row 1 (RS): [Kfb] 3 times. (6 sts)

Row 2 (WS): [Pfb, p1, pfb] twice. (10 sts)

Row 3: [Kfb, k3, kfb] twice. (14 sts)

Rows 4–7: Work in st st.

Bind off all sts. Fold ear in half and sew side seam to form half-circle. Sew bound-off edge to head and pull all loose ends into head to conceal.

BODY:

Cast on 3 sts with A.

Row 1 (RS): [Kfb] 3 times. (6 sts)

Row 2 (WS): [Pfb] 6 times. (12 sts)

Row 3: [K1, kfb] 6 times. (18 sts)

Row 4: [P2, pfb] 6 times. (24 sts)
Row 5: [K3, kfb] 6 times. (30 sts)
Row 6: [P4, pfb] 6 times. (36 sts)
Row 7: [K5, kfb] 6 times. (42 sts)
Rows 8–12: Work in st st.
Row 13: K15, [k2, k2tog] 3 times, k15. (39 sts)
Row 14: P15, [p2tog, p1] 3 times, p15. (36 sts)
Rows 15–18: Work in st st.
Row 19: K2, k2tog, [k8, k2tog] 3 times, k2. (32 sts)
Row 20 and every foll WS row: P all sts.
Row 21: K2, k2tog, k6, k2tog, k8, k2tog, k6, k2tog, k2. (28 sts)
Row 23: K2, k2tog, k4, k2tog, k8, k2tog, k4, k2tog, k2. (24 sts)
Cut A and join B.
Row 25 (RS): [K2, k2tog] twice, k8, [k2tog, k2] twice. (20 sts)
Row 27: K2, [k2tog] twice, k8, [k2tog] twice, k2. (16 sts)
Row 29: [K2tog] 8 times. (8 sts)
Row 31: [K2tog] 4 times. (4 sts)
Cut yarn, leaving a long tail, and thread onto a yarn needle. Thread yarn through remaining live sts, pull tight, and tie off. The cast-on edge will be the bottom of the body and Row 31 is at the neck. Sew up the back of the body, selvage to selvage, being sure to stuff before your seam is finished and shut. Sew to head. Secure any ends and pull them inside the body to conceal.

ARMS (make 2):
Cast on 3 sts with B.
Row 1 (RS): [Kfb] 3 times. (6 sts)
Row 2 (WS): [Pfb, p1, pfb] twice. (10 sts)
Row 3: [Kfb, k3, kfb] twice. (14 sts)
Rows 4–16: Work in st st.
Row 17 (RS): K5, [k2tog] twice, k5. (12 sts)

Row 18 and every foll WS row: P all sts.
Row 19: K4, [k2tog] twice, k4. (10 sts)
Row 21: K3, [k2tog] twice, k3. (8 sts)
Row 23: K2, [k2tog] twice, k2. (6 sts)
Row 25: K all sts.
Cut yarn, leaving a long tail, and thread onto a yarn needle. Thread yarn through remaining live sts, pull tight, and tie off. Sew up arm, stuffing lightly. Sew to shoulder, with seam facing body.

LEGS (make 2):
Cast on 3 sts with B.
Row 1 (RS): [Kfb] 3 times. (6 sts)
Row 2 (WS): [Pfb] 6 times. (12 sts)
Row 3: [K1, kfb] 6 times. (18 sts)
Row 4: [P5, pfb] 3 times. (21 sts)
Rows 5–8: Work in st st.
Row 9: K6, [k2tog] 5 times, k5. (16 sts)
Row 10: P5, [p2tog] 3 times, p5. (13 sts)
Rows 11–26: Work in st st.
Bind off all sts. Sew up the back of leg, stuff foot and leg, and sew to body

Finishing
Secure any remaining ends inside body. Wash gently and let dry.

Olaf

Olaf is a quick project, because he's knitted from super-bulky yarn on thick needles. If you're going to make him out of a dark-colored yarn, be sure to use a matching color of wool roving to stuff him with, as white fiberfill may show through the stitches.

You will need:

- Pair of US size 10 (6 mm) knitting needles
- 87 yd (80 m) of super-bulky-weight yarn
- Small amount of black worsted-weight yarn for embroidering nose and eyes
- Small amount of dark brown embroidery floss for embroidering mouth
- Small amount of white embroidery floss for embroidering highlights on eyes
- Polyester fiberfill stuffing/wool roving
- Yarn needle

Elf hat, see page 91

Sweater vest, see page 69

Stocking, see page 81   Tiny bear, see page 86

Gauge

7 sts by 8 rows = 2 in (5 cm) square in stockinette stitch

Instructions

HEAD:

Cast on 3 sts.

Row 1 (RS): [Kfb] 3 times. (6 sts)

Row 2 and all following WS rows through Row 22: P all sts.

Row 3: [Kfb] 6 times. (12 sts)

Row 5: K3, kfb, k4, kfb, k3. (14 sts)

Row 7: K4, M1, kfb, k2, M1, k2, kfb, M1, k4. (19 sts)

Row 9: K6, kfb, k5, kfb, k6. (21 sts)

Row 11: K7, kfb, k2, kfb, k2, kfb, k7. (24 sts)

Row 13: K8, kfb, k3, M1, k3, kfb, k8. (27 sts)

Row 15: K9, kfb, k3, kfb, k3, kfb, k9. (30 sts)

Row 17: K10, kfb, k4, M1, k4, kfb, k10. (33 sts)

Row 19: K11, kfb, k9, kfb, k11. (35 sts)

Row 21: K all sts.

Row 23: K11, k2tog, k9, k2tog, k11. (33 sts)

Row 24 (WS): P10, p2tog, p9, p2tog, p10. (31 sts)

Row 25: [K2tog] 7 times, k3, [k2tog] 7 times. (17 sts)

Row 26: [P2tog] 3 times, p5, [p2tog] 3 times. (11 sts)

Row 27: [K2tog] twice, k3, [k2tog] twice. (7 sts)

Cut yarn, leaving a long tail, and thread onto a yarn needle. Thread yarn through remaining live sts, pull tight, and tie off. The cast-on edge is the nose, and Row 27 is at the back of the head. Sew the head together with a seam that stretches down from the back of the head, under the neck region, then back up under the nose. Be sure to stuff the head before the seam is finished, using fingers to shape and putting extra stuffing into the snout. When the head is stuffed and sewn shut, embroider on eyes, nose, and mouth, using photo for guidance. Pull any loose ends into head to conceal.

EARS (make 2):

Cast on 5 sts.

Row 1 (RS): K all sts.

Row 2 (WS): Sl1, p1, pfb, p1, sl1. (6 sts)

Row 3: Sl1, [kfb] 4 times, sl1. (10 sts)

Row 4: P all sts.

Bind off all sts.

The ear will be shaped somewhat like a letter C. Sew to the head, knit side facing forward, so that both short ends and the cast-on edge are attached to the head.

BODY:

Cast on 10 sts.

Row 1 (RS): K all sts.

Row 2 (WS): P2, kfb, p4, kfb, p2. (12 sts)

Row 3: K4, kfb, k2, kfb, k4. (14 sts)

Row 4: P all sts.

Row 5: [K2, kfb] 4 times, k2. (18 sts)

Row 6: P all sts.

Row 7: K2, kfb, k3, kfb, k4, kfb, k3, kfb, k2. (22 sts)

Row 8: P all sts.

Row 9: K all sts.

Row 10: P all sts.

Row 11: K4, [k2tog] twice, k6, [k2tog] twice, k4. (18 sts)

Row 12: P all sts.

Row 13: K3, [k2tog] twice, k4, [k2tog] twice, k3. (14 sts)

Row 14: [P2tog] 7 times. (7 sts)

Cut yarn, leaving a long tail, and thread onto a yarn needle. Thread yarn through remaining live sts, pull tight, and tie off. The cast-on edge will be at the bottom of the body, and Row 14 is at the neck. Sew up the back of the body, selvage to selvage, being sure to stuff before your seam is finished and shut. Sew to head. Secure any ends and pull them inside the body to conceal.

ARMS (make 2):

Cast on 7 sts.

Rows 1–12: Starting with a RS row, work in st st.

Row 13 (RS): [K2tog] 3 times, k1. (4 sts)

Cut yarn, leaving a long tail, and thread onto a yarn needle. Thread yarn through remaining live sts, pull tight, and tie off. The cast-on edge is the shoulder, and Row 13 is at the paw. Sew up the arm and position the seam toward the body to keep it less visible. Stuff the arm lightly if desired, but it is not necessary as the thick yarn makes a stiff fabric. Sew to body at shoulder.

LEGS (make 2):

Cast on 10 sts.

Rows 1–10: Starting with a RS row, work in st st.

Row 11 (RS): K3, [kfb] 4 times, k3. (14 sts)

Rows 12–14: Work in st st.

Row 15: K3, [k2tog] 4 times, k3. (10 sts)

Row 16: P all sts.

Row 17: [K2tog] 5 times. (5 sts)

Cut yarn, leaving a long tail, and thread onto a yarn needle. Thread yarn through remaining live sts, pull tight, and tie off. The cast-on edge is where the leg meets the body, and Row 15 is at the top of the foot. Sew up the back of the leg, stuff, and attach to body.

Finishing

Secure any remaining ends inside body. Wash gently and let dry.

Hudson

Hudson has an inquisitive look, and his arms and legs get thicker toward the paws to make him more floppy and cuddly. He looks best when stuffed lightly, and knitted in a yarn with a slight texture.

You will need:

- Set of five US size 5 (3.75 mm) double-pointed knitting needles (dpns)
- 120 yd (110 m) of bulky-weight yarn in light brown
- Small amount of bulky-weight yarn in natural (for muzzle)
- 1 set of ½ in (12 mm) black acrylic safety eyes
- Small amount of black worsted-weight yarn for embroidering nose
- Small amount of black embroidery floss for embroidering mouth and whiskers
- Polyester fiberfill stuffing
- Yarn needle

Winter hat, see page 72

Backpack, see page 68

Overalls, see page 84

BEAR'S HEIGHT

9 in
(23 cm)

Gauge

7 sts by 11 rows = 2 in (5 cm) square in stockinette stitch

Instructions

HEAD:

With main yarn, cast on 4 sts.

Round 1: [Kfb] 4 times. Distribute sts evenly over 4 dpns and join to work in the round. (8 sts)

Round 2: [K1, kfb] 4 times. (12 sts)

Round 3: [K2, kfb] 4 times. (16 sts)

Round 4: [K3, kfb] 4 times. (20 sts)

Round 5: [Kfb, k3, kfb] 4 times. (28 sts)

Round 6: K all sts.

Round 7: [Kfb, k5, kfb] 4 times. (36 sts)

Rounds 8–22: K all sts.

Round 23: [K9, k2tog twice, k5] twice. (32 sts)

Round 24: [K9, k2tog twice, k3] twice. (28 sts)

Round 25: [K9, k2tog twice, k1] twice. (24 sts)

Round 26: [K2, k2tog] 6 times. (18 sts)

Round 27: K all sts.

Round 28: [K1, k2tog] 6 times. (12 sts)

Do not break yarn. Stuff head firmly, pushing extra stuffing into the jowl-type shaping on the sides in Rounds 23–26. Attach eyes, referring to photo for guidance.

BODY:

Round 29: K all sts.

Round 30: [Kfb, k2] 4 times. (16 sts)

Round 31: [Kfb, k4, kfb, k2] twice. (20 sts)

Rounds 32–42: K all sts.

Round 43: [K2tog, k6, k2tog] twice. (16 sts)

Round 44: [K2tog, k4, k2tog] twice. (12 sts)

Round 45: [K2tog] 6 times. (6 sts)

Stuff body. Cut yarn, leaving a long tail, and thread onto a yarn needle. Thread yarn through remaining live sts, pull tight, and tie off.

MUZZLE:

With muzzle yarn, cast on 24 sts.

Round 1: K all sts. Distribute sts evenly over 4 dpns and join to work in the round.

Round 2: [K2, k2tog] 6 times. (18 sts)

Round 3: [K1, k2tog] 6 times. (12 sts)

Round 4: [K2tog] 6 times. (6 sts)

Round 5: [K2tog] 3 times. (3 sts)

Cut yarn, leaving a long tail, and thread onto a yarn needle. Thread yarn through remaining live sts, pull tight, and tie off. Muzzle should look like a circle. Embroider a triangle-shaped nose, mouth, and whiskers on muzzle, referring to photo for guidance. Position muzzle on head and sew onto face, securing ends on inside of head.

EARS (make 2):

With main yarn, cast on 6 sts.

Row 1 (RS): K all sts.

Row 2 (WS): P3, M1, p3. (7 sts)

Row 3: K3, kfb, k3. (8 sts)

Row 4: P all sts.

Row 5: K1, k2tog, k2, k2tog, k1. (6 sts)

Row 6: P all sts.

Row 7: [K2tog] 3 times. (3 sts)

Cut yarn, leaving a long tail, and thread onto a yarn needle. Thread yarn through remaining live sts. Pull tight and, using your yarn needle, weave the end straight down from the top of the ear to the base. This will help you to round out the top of your ear. When you are satisfied with the shape of the ear, tie off end and sew cast-on edge of ear to head, with RS to front.

ARMS (make 2):

With main yarn, cast on 6 sts.

Round 1: K all sts. Distribute sts evenly over 3 dpns and join to work in the round.

Round 2: [K1, kfb, k1] twice. (8 sts)

Rounds 3–6: K all sts.

Round 7: [K2, M1, k2] twice. (10 sts)

Rounds 8–16: K all sts.

Cut yarn, leaving a long tail, and thread onto a yarn needle. Thread yarn through remaining live sts. Stuff the wide part of the arm before pulling yarn tight. This forms the lower part of the arm; leave the upper part (approx. Rounds 1–6) unstuffed to keep piece "floppy." Sew cast-on edge of arm to shoulder.

LEGS (make 2):

Work as for Arms through Round 7.

Rounds 8–11: K all sts.

Round 12: [K2, kfb, k2] twice. (12 sts)

Rounds 13–21: K all sts.

Cut yarn, leaving a long tail, and thread onto a yarn needle. Thread yarn through remaining live sts. Stuff the wide part of the leg before pulling yarn tight. This forms the lower part of the leg; leave the upper part (approx. Rounds 1–6) unstuffed to keep piece "floppy." Sew cast-on edge of leg to lower body.

Finishing

Secure any remaining ends inside body. Wash gently and let dry.

Winston

Sweet Winston gets his sleepy koala look from a few extra stitches that create eyelids. His puffy ears are knitted from a fuzzy yarn and are brushed with a wire brush to give them a furry halo.

You will need:

- Set of five US size 3 (3.25 mm) double-pointed knitting needles (dpns)
- 100 yd (92 m) of worsted-weight yarn in gray
- Small amount of alpaca-blend worsted-weight yarn in white for ears
- 1 set of ½ in (12 mm) black acrylic safety eyes
- Small amount of brown embroidery floss for embroidering mouth
- Small amount of black worsted-weight yarn for embroidering nose and paws
- Polyester fiberfill stuffing
- Slicker brush or similar wire-bristled brush
- Yarn needle

Fringed scarf, see page 75

Vest, see page 79

Blanket, see page 76

BEAR'S HEIGHT

9 in
(23 cm)

Gauge

12 sts by 14 rows = 2 in (5 cm) square in stockinette stitch

Instructions

HEAD:

With main yarn, cast on 4 sts.

Set-up round: K all sts.

Round 1: [Kfb] 4 times. Distribute sts evenly over 4 dpns and join to work in the round. (8 sts)

Round 2: K3, kfb, M1, kfb, k3. (11 sts)

Round 3: K4, [kfb] 3 times, k4. (14 sts)

Round 4: K5, kfb, k1, M1, k1, kfb, k5. (17 sts)

Round 5: K6, kfb, k1, kfb, k1, kfb, k6. (20 sts)

Round 6: K7, kfb, k2, M1, k2, kfb, k7. (23 sts)

Round 7: K8, kfb, k2, kfb, k2, kfb, k8. (26 sts)

Round 8: K9, kfb, k3, M1, k3, kfb, k9. (29 sts)

Round 9: K10, kfb, k3, kfb, k3, kfb, k10. (32 sts)

Round 10: K11, kfb, k4, M1, k4, kfb, k11. (35 sts)

Round 11: K12, kfb, k4, kfb, k4, kfb, k12. (38 sts)

Round 12: K13, kfb, k5, M1, k5, kfb, k13. (41 sts)

Round 13: K14, kfb, k5, kfb, k5, kfb, k14. (44 sts)

Round 14: K2, kfb, k12, kfb, k12, kfb, k12, kfb, k2. (48 sts)

Round 15: K3, kfb, k12, kfb, k14, kfb, k12, kfb, k3. (52 sts)

Round 16: K4, kfb, k12, kfb, k16, kfb, k12, kfb, k4. (56 sts)

Rounds 17–32: K all sts.

Round 33: K18, k2tog, k16, k2tog, k18. (54 sts)

Round 34: K17, k2tog, k16, k2tog, k17. (52 sts)

Round 35: K16, k2tog, k16, k2tog, k16. (50 sts)

Round 36: [K2tog] 25 times. (25 sts)

Stuff head firmly and attach eyes.

Round 37: [K2tog] 12 times, k1. (13 sts)

Cut yarn, leaving a long tail, and thread onto a yarn needle. Thread yarn through remaining live sts, making sure head is fully stuffed. Pull tight to close hole, tie off, and weave in ends. Embroider on nose and mouth. Using main yarn, embroider 4–5 long running stitches over top of each eye for eyelids.

EARS (make 2):

With yarn for ears, cast on 3 sts.

Round 1: [Kfb] 3 times. Distribute sts evenly over 3 dpns and join to work in the round. (6 sts)

Round 2: [Kfb] 6 times. (12 sts)

Round 3: [K1, kfb] 6 times. (18 sts)

Round 4: [K2, kfb] 6 times. (24 sts)

Rounds 5–10: K all sts.

Round 11: [K2, k2tog] 6 times. (18 sts)

Round 12: [K1, k2tog] 6 times. (12 sts)

Stuff ear lightly.

Round 13: [K2tog] 6 times. (6 sts)

Cut yarn, leaving a long tail, and thread onto a yarn needle. Thread yarn through remaining live sts, pull tight, and tie off. The ear should be a ball shape. Using slicker brush, vigorously brush the yarn first down, then to the left, then to the right, then up, then down again. This will loosen the fibers that are stuck in the stitches and pull them out to create a furry halo around the ear. Once the ear is as fuzzy as you like it, sew to head.

BODY:

With main yarn, cast on 8 sts.

Set-up round: K all sts. Distribute sts evenly over 4 dpns and join to work in the round.

Round 1: [Kfb] 8 times. (16 sts)

Round 2: [K1, kfb] 8 times. (24 sts)

Round 3: [K2, kfb] 8 times. (32 sts)

Round 4: [K3, kfb] 8 times. (40 sts)

Round 5: [K4, kfb] 8 times. (48 sts)
Rounds 6–17: K all sts.
Round 18: [K12, k2tog, k8, k2tog] twice. (44 sts)
Round 19: [K12, k2tog, k6, k2tog] twice. (40 sts)
Round 20: [K12, k2tog, k4, k2tog] twice. (36 sts)
Round 21: [K2, k2tog, k4, k2tog, k8] twice. (32 sts)
Round 22: [K2, k2tog, k2, k2tog, k8] twice. (28 sts)
Round 23: [K2, k2tog, k2tog, k8] twice. (24 sts)
Round 24: K all sts.
Round 25: [K6, k2tog, k2, k2tog] twice. (20 sts)
Round 26: [K6, k2tog twice] twice. (16 sts) Stuff body.
Rounds 27–28: K all sts.
Cut yarn and thread onto a yarn needle. Thread yarn through remaining live sts, pull tight, and tie off, making sure body is fully stuffed. Round 28 is the top of the body. Orient the body by finding the "K8" sections in Rounds 21 and 22—they are the sides of the body. Sew to head.

ARMS (make 2):
With main yarn, cast on 6 sts.
Round 1: [Kfb] 6 times. Distribute sts evenly over 3 dpns and join to work in the round. (12 sts)
Round 2: K all sts.
Round 3: [K1, kfb] 6 times. (18 sts)
Rounds 4–15: K all sts.
Round 16: Kfb, k17. (19 sts)
Rounds 17–19: K all sts.

Round 20: Kfb, k18. (20 sts)
Rounds 21–23: K all sts.
Round 24: Kfb, k19. (21 sts)
Rounds 25–27: K all sts.
Round 28: Kfb, k20. (22 sts)
Redistribute your stitches so that the first 11 sts of the row are on one dpn, and the second 11 sts are on another. The two needles should be parallel to each other. Loosely stuff arm, then join both sets of sts using three-needle bind off, leaving a long tail when you cut the yarn. Use the tail to sew the arms to the shoulders of the bear. The flat bound-off edge should sit on the bear's side diagonally—starting right where the head meets the body directly under the ear, slanting down, and toward the back. Increases in Rounds 16–28 should be at the underside of each arm. Embroider paws.

LEGS (make 2):
Work as for Arms through Round 28.
Rounds 29–31: K all sts.
Round 32: [K2tog] 11 times. (11 sts)
Stuff leg. Cut yarn and thread onto a yarn needle. Thread yarn through remaining live sts, pull tight, and tie off. Increases in Rounds 16–28 form a line at the top of the leg. Position legs with this line facing up; sew to hips in a seated position. Embroider paws.

Finishing
Secure any remaining ends inside body. Wash gently and let dry.

Bridget

Bridget is a sweet bear with a vintage look. Her unique ribbed appearance is due to being knitted in garter stitch. She is knitted flat and then sewn up, which makes her an ideal project for someone who doesn't want to use double-pointed needles.

Beret, see page 78

Sweater vest, see page 69

Skirt, see page 80

BEAR'S HEIGHT

10 in
(25.5 cm)

Gauge

11 sts by 13 rows = 2 in (5 cm) square in garter stitch (knit every row), slightly stretched

Instructions

HEAD:

Cast on 6 sts.

Row 1: [Kfb] 6 times. (12 sts)

Row 2: [Kfb, k4, kfb] twice. (16 sts)

Row 3: [Kfb, k2, kfb, k4] twice. (20 sts)

Row 4: [Kfb, k4, kfb, k4] twice. (24 sts)

Rows 5–8: K all sts.

Row 9: K7, [kfb] twice, k1, kfb, k2, kfb, k1, [kfb] twice, k7. (30 sts)

Row 10: K10, kfb, k1, kfb, k4, kfb, k1, kfb, k10. (34 sts)

Row 11: K8, [kfb] twice, k4, kfb, k4, kfb, k4, [kfb] twice, k8. (40 sts)

Row 12: K all sts.

Row 13: K10, kfb, k18, kfb, k10. (42 sts)

Row 14: K11, kfb, k18, kfb, k11. (44 sts)

Row 15: K12, kfb, k18, kfb, k12. (46 sts)

Row 16: K13, kfb, k18, kfb, k13. (48 sts)

Row 17: K14, kfb, k18, kfb, k14. (50 sts)

Rows 18–33: K all sts.

Row 34: K14, [k2tog] twice, k14, [k2tog] twice, k14. (46 sts)

Row 35: K12, [k2tog] twice, k14, [k2tog] twice, k12. (42 sts)

Row 36: K10, [k2tog] twice, k14, [k2tog] twice, k10. (38 sts)

Row 37: [K2tog] 19 times. (19 sts)

Row 38: [K2tog] 9 times, k1. (10 sts)

Row 39: [K2tog] 5 times. (5 sts)

Cut yarn, leaving a long tail, and thread onto a yarn needle. Thread yarn through remaining live sts, pull tight, and tie off. The cast-on edge is the nose, and Row 39 is at the back of the head.

Sew the head together with a seam that stretches down from the back of the head, under the neck region, then back up under the nose; when the seam is half-completed, attach eyes, and when there is approximately a 1-in (3-cm) opening left, stuff the head firmly. Complete seam. Embroider on nose and mouth, using photo for guidance.

EARS (make 2):

Cast on 14 sts.

Rows 1–4: K all sts.

Row 5: [K2tog, k3, k2tog] twice. (10 sts)

Row 6: [K2tog, k1, k2tog] twice. (6 sts)

Row 7: [K2tog] 3 times. (3 sts)

Cut yarn, leaving a long tail, and thread onto a yarn needle. Thread yarn through remaining live sts. Pull tight and sew edges together, from top to bottom. Press ear so that the seam runs down the middle back of the ear. Sew to head.

BODY:

Cast on 6 sts.

Row 1: K all sts. (6 sts)

Row 2: [Kfb] 6 times. (12 sts)

Row 3: [K1, kfb] 6 times. (18 sts)

Row 4: [K2, kfb] 6 times. (24 sts)

Row 5: [K3, kfb] 6 times. (30 sts)

Row 6: [K4, kfb] 6 times. (36 sts)

Row 7: [K5, kfb] 6 times. (42 sts)

Rows 8–18: K all sts.

Row 19: [K5, k2tog] 6 times. (36 sts)

Row 20 and every following even row through Row 28: K all sts.

Row 21: [K4, k2tog] 6 times. (30 sts)

Row 23: [K3, k2tog] 6 times. (24 sts)

Row 25: [K2, k2tog] 6 times. (18 sts)

Row 27: [K1, k2tog] 6 times. (12 sts)

Row 29: [K2tog] 6 times. (6 sts)

Bind off remaining sts. The cast-on edge will be the bottom of the body, and Row 29 is at the neck. Sew up the back of the body, selvage to selvage, being sure to stuff before your seam is finished and shut. Secure any ends and pull them inside the body to conceal. Roll the body between your hands gently to give it a nice, smooth, teardrop shape. Sew bound-off edge to head.

ARMS (make 2):

Cast on 7 sts.

Row 1: [Kfb] 7 times. (14 sts)

Rows 2–22: K all sts.

Row 23: K1, k2tog, k3, k2tog, k3, k2tog, k1. (11 sts)

Row 24: K all sts.

Row 25: K1, k2tog, k1, sl1, k2tog, psso, k1, k2tog, k1. (7 sts)

Rows 26–28: K all sts.

Row 29: K2, sl1, k2tog, psso, k2. (5 sts)

Rows 30–31: K all sts.

Row 32: K1, sl1, k2tog, psso, k1. (3 sts)

Cut yarn, leaving a long tail, and thread onto a yarn needle. Thread yarn through remaining 3 sts. Pull tight to tie off. Use long tail to sew the selvage edges of the arm together. The skinny part at Rows 25–32 is the top of the arm (shoulder) and the cast-on edge is at the end of the paw. Stuff the arm as you sew it up, but be careful not to overstuff—the garter stitch fabric will have a tendency to stretch out. Combat this by stuffing lightly and rolling between your hands to evenly distribute the stuffing when the arm is done. Sew the arm on, with the seam facing in toward the body.

LEGS (make 2):

Cast on 14 sts.

Rows 1–16: K all sts.

Row 17: K5, [kfb] 4 times, k5. (18 sts)

Rows 18–22: K all sts.

Row 23: K5, [k2tog] 4 times, k5. (14 sts)

Row 24: [K2tog] 7 times. (7 sts)

Row 25: [K2tog] 3 times, k1. (4 sts)

Row 26: [K2tog] twice. (2 sts)

Cut yarn, leaving a long tail, and thread onto a yarn needle. Thread yarn through remaining live sts, pull tight, and tie off. The increases at Row 17 will form the top of the foot, and Row 26 is the bottom of the foot. Sew the edges together with the long tail, leaving the top of the leg open to stuff. Stuff the leg, making sure to push extra stuffing into the foot and shape it carefully. Sew the cast-on edge of the leg to the bottom of the body.

Finishing

Secure any remaining ends inside body. Wash gently and let dry.

Accessory patterns

Backpack

You will need:
- Pair of US size 5 (3.75 mm) knitting needles
- 50 yd (46 m) of worsted-weight yarn
- Yarn needle

FRONT

Gauge

13 sts by 20 rows = 2 in (5 cm) in pattern stitch

Note

The slipped stitch pattern on this piece creates a woven-look fabric that gives the backpack a sturdy quality and does not stretch.

INSTRUCTIONS
FRINGE:

Cast on 15 sts.

Row 1 (WS): Purl.

Row 2 (RS): K1, [k1, sl1 wyif] 6 times, k2.

Row 3 (WS): [P1, sl1 wyib] 7 times, p1.

Repeat Rows 2–3 ten times more. Work measures approx. 2¼ in (5.5 cm) from CO.

Shape sides and bottom:

Row 24 (RS): K1, [k1, sl1 wyif] 6 times, k2, CO 15 sts at end of row. Turn. (30 sts)

Row 25: P15, [p1, sl1 wyib] 7 times, p1, CO 15 sts at end of row. Turn. (45 sts)

Row 26: K16, [k1, sl1 wyif] 14 times, k1.

Row 27 (WS): P2, [sl1 wyib, p1] 21 times, p1.

Row 28 (RS): [K1, sl1 wyif] 22 times, k1.

BACK

Repeat Rows 27–28 twice more. Piece measures approx. 3¼ in (8 cm) from first cast-on edge.

Row 33 (WS): Bind off 15 sts (1 st remaining on RH needle from bind off), [sl1 wyib, p1] 14 times, p1. (30 sts)
Row 34 (RS): Bind off 15 sts (1 st remaining on RH needle from bind off), [k1, sl1 wyif] 6 times, k2. (15 sts)

BACK:
Row 35 (WS): [P1, sl1 wyib] 7 times, p1.
Row 36 (RS): K1, [k1, sl1 wyif] 6 times, k2.
Repeat Rows 35–36 ten times more. Work measures approx. 2¼ in (5.5 cm) from bound-off edges.

FLAP:
Row 57 (folding row—WS): Knit.
Row 58 (RS): Sl1 wyif, [k1, sl1 wyif] 7 times.
Row 59: [P1, sl1 wyib] 7 times, p1.
Repeat Rows 58–59 four times more, then rep Row 58 once more.

Row 69 (folding row—WS): Knit.
Repeat Rows 58–59 seven times more. Bind off all sts knit-wise.

Finishing
The piece will resemble a lower-case "t," with the flap at the bottom and the first cast-on edge at the top. Sew the cast-on edges of Rows 24–25 to the side edges of the front of the bag. Sew the bound-off edges of Rows 33–34 to the side edges of the back of the bag. Let the flap naturally fold over the top of the bag. Wash gently and lay flat to dry if desired.

STRAPS:
With the back of the backpack facing, pick up and knit 3 sts from back, picking up from 1 st to right of center, just below Row 57 (folding row). *Slip all 3 sts back to LH needle. K3. Do not turn. Rep from * until strap measures 4 in (10 cm) long. Cut yarn, pull through remaining sts, sew to the bottom right corner of the back. Rep for other strap, picking up sts 1 st to left of center and sewing end to bottom left corner of the back. Weave in ends.

Sweater vest

You will need:
- Set of five US size 5 (3.75 mm) double-pointed knitting needles (dpns)
- 25 yd (23 m) of worsted-weight yarn
- Small amount of worsted-weight yarn in contrasting color (optional)
- Waste yarn
- Yarn needle

Gauge
11 sts by 16 rows = 2 in (5 cm) square in stockinette stitch For the striped version of this vest, attach CC (contrast color) yarn on Round 3, leaving MC (main color) yarn still attached. Alternate these two colors, using CC on even rows.

INSTRUCTIONS
BODY:
Cast on 42 sts. Distribute sts evenly over 3 dpns and join to work in the round.

Rounds 1–3: [K1, p1] 21 times.
Rounds 4–13: Knit.
Round 14: Bind off 2 sts, k20 (for 21 sts on needle after bind off), place remaining 19 sts of round on waste yarn. Turn.

FRONT:

Row 1 (WS): Bind off 2 sts, purl to end. (19 sts)
Row 2: K1, k2tog, k13, k2tog, k1. (17 sts)
Row 3: Purl.

LEFT FRONT:

Row 4 (RS): K7, k2tog, turn. (8 sts)
Row 5: Purl.
Row 6: Knit to last 3 sts, k2tog, k1. (1 st decreased)
Rows 7–10: Repeat Rows 5–6 twice more. (5 sts)
Bind off 5 remaining sts.

RIGHT FRONT:

With RS facing, join yarn to rem 8 sts of front.
Row 4 (RS): K2tog, k6. (7 sts)
Row 5: Purl.
Row 6: K1, k2tog, knit to end. (6 sts)
Row 7: Purl.
Rows 8–9: Repeat Rows 6–7 once more. (5 sts)
Bind off 5 remaining sts.

BACK:

Join yarn to 19 sts held for Back with RS facing.
Row 1 (RS): Bind off 2 sts, knit to end. (17 sts)
Row 2: Bind off 2 sts, purl to end. (15 sts)
Row 3: K1, k2tog, knit to last 3 sts, k2tog, k1. (2 sts decreased)
Row 4: Purl.
Rows 5–6: Repeat Rows 3–4 once more. (11 sts)
Row 7: Knit.
Bind off all sts.

Finishing

Sew bound-off edge of shoulders to back, leaving back neck approximately 1 in (2.5 cm) wide and gathering shoulders slightly in seam. If desired, apply chart to front of vest using contrasting color and duplicate stitch. Weave in ends. Wash gently and lay flat to dry if desired.

CHART

Dress

You will need:
- Pair of US size 3 (3.25 mm) needles
- 70 yd (65 m) of fingering-weight yarn
- Yarn needle

Gauge

13 sts by 17 rows = 2 in (5 cm) square in stockinette stitch

INSTRUCTIONS

Cast on 28 sts.

Rows 1–2: [K1, p1] 14 times.

Row 3 (RS): K6, M1, k1, M1, k14, M1, k1, M1, k6. (32 sts)

Row 4 and every foll WS row through Row 14: Purl.

Row 5: K7, [M1, k1] 3 times, M1, k12, [M1, k1] 3 times, M1, k7. (40 sts)

Row 7: K8, M1, k1, M1, k3, M1, k1, M1, k14, M1, k1, M1, k3, M1, k1, M1, k8. (48 sts)

Row 9: K9, M1, k1, M1, k5, M1, k1, M1, k16, M1, k1, M1, k5, M1, k1, M1, k9. (56 sts)

Row 11: K10, M1, k1, M1, k7, M1, k1, M1, k18, M1, k1, M1, k7, M1, k1, M1, k10. (64 sts)

Row 13: K11, M1, k1, M1, k9, M1, k1, M1, k20, M1, k1, M1, k9, M1, k1, M1, k11. (72 sts)

Row 15: K13, Bind off 11 sts for first sleeve, k23 (for 24 sts on needle after first bind off), bind off 11 sts for second sleeve, knit to end. (50 sts)

Row 16: P13, cast on 4 sts, p24, cast on 4 sts, p13. (58 sts)

Row 17: Knit.

Row 18: Purl.

Row 19: [K3, M1] 19 times, k1. (77 sts)

Continue in st st for 18 rows more, or to desired length. Bind off all sts.

Finishing

Sew seam in center back of dress using mattress stitch. Weave in ends. Wash gently and lay flat to dry if desired.

Winter hat

Gauge

7 sts by 11 rows = 2 in (5 cm) square in double seed stitch

DOUBLE SEED STITCH PATTERN:

Row 1: [K2, p2] to end.
Row 2: [K2, p2] to end.
Row 3: [P2, k2] to end.
Row 4: [P2, k2] to end.

INSTRUCTIONS

Cast on 48 sts.
Rows 1–3: K1, p1 to end.
Rows 4–5: Work in double seed stitch pattern.
Ear holes: Working in pattern, k 10 sts. Put remaining sts on a holder and continue to work just these 10 sts in pattern for 7 rows. Now put these sts on a holder, cut yarn, attach to next sts, and work the next 28 sts in the same way for 7 rows. Put the middle 28 sts on a holder and work the last 10 sts for 7 rows. At the end of this row, you should have all three sections the same length, with two slit-shaped ear holes between them. Work in double seed stitch pattern for another 8 rows.

Begin to decrease for top of hat:
[K2tog, p2tog] to end of row (24 sts).
Work in pattern on WS.
[K2tog] to end of row (12 sts).
Cut yarn; use a yarn needle to pull through remaining live stitches. Pull tight to gather the top of the hat.

Finishing

Using mattress stitch, sew up the back seam of the hat, tie off, and weave in ends. Wash gently and lay flat to dry if desired. Make a 2- to 3-inch (5- to 7.5-cm) pom-pom and attach to top of hat.

Beanie

Gauge

21 sts by 18 rows = 2 in (5 cm) square in K2, P2 rib, relaxed

INSTRUCTIONS

Cast on 72 sts. Distribute sts evenly over 4 dpns and join to work in the round.

Round 1: [K2, p2] 18 times.

Rep Round 1 until piece measures 2½ in (6.5 cm) from cast on.

EAR HOLE

Round 1: [K2, p2] 3 times, bind off 8 sts, [k2, p2] 6 times (including st leftover from bind off), bind off 8 sts, work in pattern to end of round.

Round 2: [K2, p2] 3 times, cast on 8 sts, [k2, p2] 6 times, cast on 8 sts, [k2, p2] to end.

Work in [k2, p2] rib for 1 in (2.5 cm) more.

Next round: [K2, p2tog] 18 times. (54 sts)

Next round: [K2, p1] 18 times.

Next round: [K2tog, p1] 18 times. (36 sts)

Next round: [K2tog] 18 times. (18 sts)

Next round: [K2tog] 9 times. (9 sts)

Cut yarn, leaving a long tail, and thread onto a yarn needle. Thread yarn through remaining sts, and tie off.

Finishing

Weave any loose ends into hat to conceal. Wash gently and lay flat to dry if desired.

Cardigan

You will need:

- Pair of US size 5 (3.75 mm) needles
- Set of four US size 5 (3.75 mm) double-pointed knitting needles (dpns)
- 55 yd (50 m) of worsted-weight yarn
- Waste yarn
- Yarn needle
- Four ½ in (12 mm) buttons
- Sewing needle and thread

Gauge

11 sts by 13.5 rows = 2 in (5 cm) square in stockinette stitch

INSTRUCTIONS
BODY:

With straight needles, cast on 50 sts.

Row 1 (RS): [K1, p1] 25 times.

Row 2: [P1, k1] 25 times.

Row 3: K1, p1, knit to last 3 sts, p1, k1, p1.

Row 4 and every foll WS row through Row 18: P1, k1, purl to last 3 sts, k1, p1, k1.

Rows 5–10: Repeat Rows 3–4 three times more.

Row 11: K1, p1, k10, k3tog, k19, k3tog, k10, p1, k1, p1. (46 sts)

Row 13: K1, p1, k9, k3tog, k17, k3tog, k9, p1, k1, p1. (42 sts)

Row 15: K1, p1, k8, k3tog, k15, k3tog, k8, p1, k1, p1. (38 sts)

Row 17: K1, p1, k7, k3tog, k13, k3tog, k7, p1, k1, p1. (34 sts)

Row 19: K1, p1, k5, bind off 6 sts, k7 (for a total of 8 sts on RH needle after last bind off), bind off 6 sts, k3 (for a total of 4 sts on RH needle after last bind off), p1, k1, p1.

LEFT FRONT:

Row 20 (WS): P1, k1, p1, p2, p2tog, turn. Leave rem sts of row on waste yarn, if desired. (6 sts)

Row 21 (RS): K3, p1, ssk. (5 sts)

Row 22: K1, p1, p3.

Row 23: K3, p1, k1.

Rep Rows 22–23 once more. Bind off.

BACK:

With WS facing, place next 8 held sts on needle and join yarn.

Row 20 (WS): P8.

Row 21: K2tog, k4, k2tog. (6 sts)

Cont in st st for 4 rows more. Bind off.

RIGHT FRONT:

With WS facing, place next 7 sts on needle and join yarn.

Row 20 (WS): P2tog, p2, k1, p1, k1. (6 sts)

Row 21: P2tog, k4. (5 sts)

Row 22: P3, k1, p1.

Row 23: P1, k4.

Rep Rows 22–23 once more. Bind off.

SLEEVES:

Sew 2 sts of left front closest to armhole to back shoulder. Repeat for right shoulder. This will leave 3 bound-off sts for each front for collar.

With dpns and RS facing, pick up and knit 16 sts around first armhole. Distribute sts evenly over 3 dpns and join to work in the round.

Knit 20 rounds. Bind off. Repeat for other sleeve.

COLLAR:

With RS facing, pick up and knit 5 sts from right front, 8 sts from back, and 5 sts from left front. (18 sts)

Knit 4 rows. Bind off.

Finishing

Weave in ends. Block gently. Sew on buttons evenly spaced to left front buttonband. Wash gently and lay flat to dry if desired.

FRONT

BACK

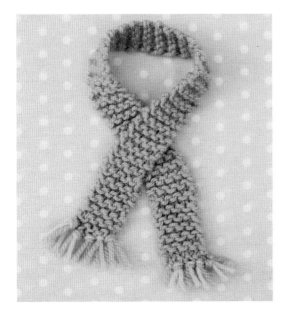

Fringed scarf

You will need:
- Pair of US size 5 (3.75 mm) knitting needles
- 25 yd (23 m) of worsted-weight yarn
- US size F-5 (3.75 mm) crochet hook
- Yarn needle

Gauge

5 sts by 8 rows = 1 in (2.5 cm) square in garter stitch (knit every row), relaxed

INSTRUCTIONS

Cast on 5 sts.
Knit 110 rows.
Bind off all sts.

Finishing

Weave in ends. Wash gently and lay flat to dry if desired.

FRINGE:

Cut 20 pieces of yarn approximately 3 in (8 cm) long. Take two pieces of fringe and the crochet hook. Fold the pieces of fringe in half. Push crochet hook through first bound-off st. Hook the two pieces of fringe where they are folded in half, and pull them back through the st so that they create a loop approximately 1 in (2.5 cm) high. Pull the ends of the fringe through this loop and pull tight. Repeat for 4 remaining bound-off sts and for cast-on edge. Trim fringe to approximately ¾ in (2 cm) long on each side.

Blanket

You will need:

- Pair of US size 4 (3.5 mm) knitting needles
- 25 yd (23 m) of fingering-weight yarn in pink (color A)
- 25 yd (23 m) of fingering-weight yarn in green (color B)
- Yarn needle

Gauge

20 sts = 3 in (7.5 cm) in pattern stitch

Note

Do not carry color B up side of work; join yarn for each stripe.

INSTRUCTIONS

Cast on 42 sts with A.
Rows 1–2: Knit.
Row 3 (RS): With A, [k1, sl1 wyif] 20 times, k2.
Row 4: With A, [p1, sl1 wyib] 20 times, p2.
Rows 5–8: Repeat Rows 3–4 twice more.
Row 9: With B, [k1, sl1 wyif] 20 times, k2.
Row 10: With B, [p1, sl1 wyib] 20 times, p2.
Repeat Rows 3–10 seven times more, then repeat Rows 3–8 once more.
Knit 2 rows in A.
Bind off all sts knit-wise.

Finishing

Block blanket and weave in ends. Wash gently and lay flat to dry if desired.

Pinafore

You will need:

- Set of five US size 5 (3.75 mm) double-pointed knitting needles (dpns)
- 25 yd (23 m) of worsted-weight yarn
- Yarn needle

Special stitch

Inc1 (eyelet increase): Pick up 1 st from bar between last st on RH needle and first st on LH needle (do not twist bar shut).

INSTRUCTIONS
SKIRT:

Cast on 28 sts. Distribute sts evenly over 4 dpns and join to work in the round.
Round 1: [K1, p1] 14 times.

Round 2: [P1, k1] 14 times.
Rep last 2 rounds once more.
Round 5: [Inc1, k4] 7 times. (35 sts)
Rounds 6–8: Knit.
Round 9: [Inc1, k5] 7 times. (42 sts)
Rounds 10–13: Knit.
Round 14: [Inc1, k6] 7 times. (49 sts)
Rounds 15–18: Knit.
Bind off.

BODICE:

Choose the section that you want to appear as the front, then flatten the skirt (Rounds 1–4 form the waistband). With RS facing, and centering stitches in front, pick up and knit 10 sts from cast-on edge (1 st in each cast-on st).
Row 2 (WS): K1, p8, k1.
Row 3: Knit.
Rep last 2 rows three times more. Bind off.

STRAPS:

With RS of front facing, pick up and knit 2 sts from top right corner of bodice. *Do not turn. Slide sts to other end of dpn and k2. Repeat from * until strap measures 2½ in (6.5 cm) from pick-up point. Bind off, leaving a long tail.
Repeat once more, picking up sts from top left corner of bodice.

Finishing

With RS of back facing, cross straps over each other and sew to waistband of skirt. Block. Weave in ends. Wash gently and lay flat to dry if desired.

FRONT

BACK

Beret

Gauge

6.5 sts by 9 rows = 1 in (2.5 cm) square in stockinette stitch

INSTRUCTIONS

Cast on 60 sts, distribute sts evenly over 4 dpns, and join to work in the round.

Rounds 1–4: [K1, p1] 30 times.

Round 5: [Kfb, k5] 10 times. (70 sts)

Round 6: [Kfb, k6] 10 times. (80 sts)

Rounds 7–12: Knit.

Round 13: [K2tog, k14, pm] 5 times. (75 sts)

Round 14: [K2tog, knit to marker] 5 times. (5 sts decreased)

Rounds 15–26: Rep Round 14 12 more times.

Round 27: [K2tog] 5 times, removing markers. (5 sts)

Cut yarn, leaving a long tail, and thread onto a yarn needle. Thread yarn through remaining live sts, pull tight, and tie off.

Finishing

Weave in ends. Block beret over a circular piece of cardboard. Wash gently and lay flat to dry if desired.

FRONT

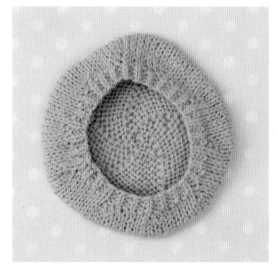

BACK

Vest

Gauge

12 sts by 18 rows = 2 in (5 cm) square in stockinette stitch

INSTRUCTIONS

Cast on 48 sts.

Row 1 (WS): Knit.

Row 2: K1, kfb, sk2p, knit to last 6 sts, sk2p, k1, kfb, k1. (2 sts decreased)

Rep last 2 rows once more. (44 sts)

Row 5: Purl.

Row 6: K1, kfb, sk2p, knit to last 6 sts, sk2p, k1, kfb, k1. (42 sts)

Rows 9–17: Work in st st.

Row 18: K1, k2tog, k7, turn, leaving remaining sts of row on waste yarn if desired.

RIGHT FRONT:

Row 19 (WS): Bind off 2 sts, purl to end. (7 sts)

Row 20: K1, k2tog, knit to end. (1 st decreased)

Row 21: Purl.

Rep Rows 20–21 once more, then rep Row 20 once more. (4 sts)

Bind off 4 remaining sts.

BACK:

With RS facing, place next 22 held sts back on LH needle, leaving rem 10 sts on holder for left front. Join yarn.

Row 18 (RS): Bind off 2 sts, knit to end, turn. (20 sts)

Row 19: Bind off 2 sts, purl to end. (18 sts)

Rows 20–24: Work in st st.

Bind off 18 remaining sts.

LEFT FRONT:

With RS facing, place rem 10 sts on LH needle and join yarn.

Row 18 (RS): Bind off 2 sts, knit to last 3 sts, k2tog, k1. (7 sts)

Row 19: Purl.

Row 20: Knit to last 3 sts, k2tog, k1. (1 st decreased)

Rep Rows 19–20 twice more. (4 sts)

Bind off 4 remaining sts.

Finishing

Block vest. Sew shoulders. Use a few stitches to secure the left front over the right front. Sew on buttons to front. Weave in ends and block gently. Wash gently and lay flat to dry if desired.

Skirt

Gauge

13 sts by 20 rows = 2 in (5 cm) in stockinette stitch

LACE PATTERN (worked in the round):
Round 1: *K1, yo, k2tog, k3, k2tog, yo; rep from * for pattern.
Rounds 2, 4, and 6: Knit.
Round 3: *K2, yo, k2tog, k1, k2tog, yo, k1; rep from * for pattern.
Round 5: *K3, yo, sk2p, yo, k2; rep from * for pattern.
Rep Rounds 1–6 for pattern.

LACE PATTERN (worked flat):
Row 1: *K1, yo, k2tog, k3, k2tog, yo; rep from * for pattern.
Rows 2, 4, and 6: Purl.
Row 3: *K2, yo, k2tog, k1, k2tog, yo, k1; rep from * for pattern.
Row 5: *K3, yo, sl1, k2tog, psso, yo, k2; rep from * for pattern.
Rep Rows 1–6 for pattern.

INSTRUCTIONS

Cast on 48 sts, distribute sts evenly over dpns, and join to work in the round.
Rounds 1–4: [K1, p1] 24 times.
Rounds 5–14: Knit.
Round 15: [K5, kfb] 8 times. (56 sts)
Rounds 16–20: Knit.
Rounds 20–25: Work Rounds 1–6 of Lace Pattern.
Bind off all sts.

Finishing

Weave in ends. Wash gently and lay flat to dry if desired.

Sleeping bag

Gauge

11 sts by 12.5 rows = 2 in (5 cm) square in stockinette stitch

Special stitches

C4B: Cable 4 back. Slip next 2 sts onto a cable needle, hold to the back, knit the next 2 sts, then knit the sts off the cable needle.

C6B: Cable 6 back. Slip the next 3 sts onto a cable needle, hold to the back, knit the next 3 sts, then knit the sts off the cable needle.

INSTRUCTIONS
Cast on 30 sts.

FRONT:
Rows 1–4: Knit.
Row 5 (RS): P4, k4, p4, k6, p4, k4, p4.
Row 6: K4, p4, k4, p6, k4, p4, k4.
Rows 7–8: Rep Rows 5–6 once more.
Row 9: P4, C4B, p4, C6B, p4, C4B, p4.
Row 10: K4, p4, k4, p6, k4, p4, k4.
Row 11: P4, k4, p4, k6, p4, k4, p4.
Row 12: K4, p4, k4, p6, k4, p4, k4.
Repeat Rows 5–12 three times more.

Sleeping bag turning row (RS): Purl.

BACK AND PILLOW:
Starting with a WS row, work in st st for 8½ in (21.5 cm), ending after a WS row.
Pillow turning row (RS): Purl.
Work in st st for 3½ in (9 cm) more.
Bind off all sts.

Finishing
Fold cast-on edge up at sleeping bag turning row so wrong sides are together. Sew sides of sleeping bag. Fold down bound-off edge at pillow turning row, sew sides, and sew down bound-off edge, stuffing before completing seam. Block into a rectangle shape and weave in ends. Wash gently and lay flat to dry if desired.

Stocking

You will need:
- Set of five US size 5 (3.75 mm) double-pointed knitting needles (dpns)
- Small amount of worsted-weight yarn in red or green (color A)
- Small amount of worsted-weight yarn in natural (color B)
- Yarn needle

Gauge
11 sts by 16 rows = 2 in (5 cm) square in stockinette stitch

Note
Stripe Pattern:
Round 1: Knit in A.
Round 2: Knit in B.
Rep last 2 rounds for pattern.

For solid stocking, work only with A except for ribbing (Rounds 1–3), heel, and toe (Round 22 to end), which are worked with B.

INSTRUCTIONS

Cast on 20 sts with A. Distribute sts evenly over dpns and join to work in the rnd.

Rounds 1–3: [K1, p1] around.

Join B and work in Stripe Pattern for 11 rounds.

Working with A only, work heel as follows:

Row 1 (RS): K8, w&t.
Row 2 (WS): P7, w&t.
Row 3: K6, w&t.
Row 4: P5, w&t.
Row 5: K4, w&t.
Row 6: P3, w&t.
Row 7: K2, w&t.
Row 8: P1, w&t.
Row 9: K2, w&t.
Row 10: P3, w&t.
Row 11: K4, w&t.
Row 12: P5, w&t.
Row 13: K6, w&t.
Row 14: P7, w&t.
Row 15 (RS): Knit to end of round.

Beginning with Round 2 of pattern, work in Stripe Pattern for 7 rounds.

Cut B and continue with A only.

Round 23: K9, k2tog, k7, k2tog. (18 sts)
Round 24: [K2tog, k5, k2tog] twice. (14 sts)
Round 25: [K2tog, k3, k2tog] twice. (10 sts)
Round 26: [K2tog, k1, k2tog] twice. (6 sts)
Bind off all sts and cut yarn, leaving a long tail. Thread tail onto yarn needle and sew toe of stocking shut.

Finishing

Embroider chart on leg using duplicate stitch. Weave in ends. Wash gently and lay flat to dry if desired.

CHART

Cardigan with lace trim

Gauge

13 sts by 20 rows = 2 in (5 cm) in stockinette stitch

LACE PATTERN (worked in the round):

Round 1: *K1, yo, k2tog, k3, k2tog, yo; rep from * for pattern.
Rounds 2, 4, and 6: Knit.
Round 3: *K2, yo, k2tog, k1, k2tog, yo, k1; rep from * for pattern.
Round 5: *K3, yo, sk2p, yo, k2; rep from * for pattern.
Rep Rounds 1–6 for pattern.

LACE PATTERN (worked flat):

Row 1: *K1, yo, k2tog, k3, k2tog, yo; rep from * for pattern.
Rows 2, 4 & 6: Purl.
Row 3: *K2, yo, k2tog, k1, k2tog, yo, k1; rep from * for pattern.
Row 5: *K3, yo, sl1, k2tog, psso, yo, k2; rep from * for pattern.
Rep Rows 1–6 for pattern.

INSTRUCTIONS
YOKE:

Cast on 24 sts.
Rows 1–4: [K1, p1] 12 times.
Row 5 (RS): Kfb, k4, M1, k2, M1, k10, M1, k2, M1, k4, kfb. (30 sts)
Row 6 and every foll WS row: Purl.

Row 7: K1, kfb, k4, M1, k1, M1, k2, M1, k1, M1, k10, M1, k1, M1, k2, M1, k1, M1, k4, kfb, k1. (40 sts)
Row 9: K1, kfb, k6, M1, k1, M1, k4, M1, k1, M1, k12, M1, k1, M1, k4, M1, k1, M1, k6, kfb, k1. (50 sts)
Row 11: K1, kfb, k8, M1, k1, M1, k6, M1, k1, M1, k14, M1, k1, M1, k6, M1, k1, M1, k8, kfb, k1. (60 sts)
Row 13: K12, place next 10 sts on holder, cast on 2 sts, k16, place next 10 sts on holder, cast on 2 sts, k12. (44 sts)
Row 14 (WS): Purl.

BODY:

Row 15 (RS): Knit.
Row 17: K1, kfb, knit to last 2 sts, kfb, k1. (46 sts)
Row 19: K1, kfb, knit to last 2 sts, kfb, k1. (48 sts)
Rows 21–26: Work Rows 1–6 of Lace Pattern.
Bind off all sts.

SLEEVES:

Knit across 10 sts held for first sleeve, pick up and knit 5 sts from underarm. Distribute sts evenly over 3 dpns and join to work in the round. (15 sts)
Knit 5 rounds.
Bind off all sts. Repeat for other sleeve.

Finishing

Weave in ends. Wash gently and lay flat to dry if desired.

Shorts

Gauge

11 sts by 17 rows = 2 in (5 cm) square in stockinette stitch

INSTRUCTIONS

Cast on 32 sts, distribute sts evenly over 4 dpns, and join to work in the round.

Rounds 1–3: [K1, p1] 16 times.

Rounds 4–15: Knit.

Round 16: K16; place remaining sts on a piece of waste yarn.

FIRST LEG:

Distribute remaining 16 sts over 4 dpns and join to work in the round. Knit 4 rounds over these 16 sts. Bind off all sts.

SECOND LEG:

Distribute 16 held sts over 4 dpns and join yarn. Complete as for First Leg.

Finishing

Stitch together any hole formed between legs. Weave in ends. Wash gently and lay flat to dry if desired.

Overalls

Gauge

13 sts by 18 rows = 2 in (5 cm) square in stockinette stitch

INSTRUCTIONS

Cast on 42 sts, distribute sts evenly over 3 dpns, and join to work in the round.

Round 1: [K1, p1] 21 times.

Round 2: [P1, k1] 21 times.

Rounds 3–6: Repeats Rounds 1–2 twice more.

Rounds 7–17: Knit.

Round 18: K21; place remaining sts on a piece of waste yarn.

FIRST LEG:

Distribute remaining 21 sts evenly over 3 dpns and join to work in the round. Knit 21 rounds over these 21 sts. Bind off all sts.

SECOND LEG:

Distribute 21 held sts over 4 dpns and join yarn. Complete as for First Leg.

BIB:

Flatten pants and choose preferred front. Centering stitches in front, pick up and knit 14 sts from cast-on edge (1 st in each cast-on st). Starting with a WS row, work in st st for 12 rows. Bind off.

STRAPS:

With RS of front facing, pick up and knit 2 sts from top right corner of Bib. *Do not turn. Slide sts to other end of dpn and k2. Repeat from * until strap measures 2½ in (6.5 cm) from pick-up point. Bind off, leaving a long tail. Repeat once more, picking up sts from top left corner of bib.

Finishing

With RS of back facing, cross straps over each other and sew to waistband of pants, using photo for guidance. Stitch together any hole formed between legs. Weave in ends. Wash gently and lay flat to dry if desired.

FRONT

BACK

Tiny bear

Gauge

5 sts by 8 rows = 1 in (2.5 cm) square in stockinette stitch

INSTRUCTIONS

HEAD:

With B, cast on 3 sts.
Round 1: [Kfb] 3 times. Distribute sts evenly over 3 dpns and join to work in the round. (6 sts)
Round 2: K1, kfb, k1, M1, k1, kfb, k1. (9 sts)
Cut B and join A.
Round 3: K2, kfb, [k1, kfb] twice, k2. (12 sts)
Round 4: K3, kfb, k2, M1, k2, kfb, k3. (15 sts)
Round 5: K4, kfb, k5, kfb, k4. (17 sts)
Round 6: [K5, kfb] twice, k5. (19 sts)
Rounds 7–13: Knit.
Round 14: [K2tog] 4 times, k3, [k2tog] 4 times. (11 sts)
Stuff head.
Round 15: [K2tog] twice, k3, [k2tog] twice. (7 sts)
Cut yarn, thread yarn onto yarn needle, thread through remaining live sts, and tie off.
Embroider on nose and eyes with embroidery floss, using photo for guidance.

EARS

Cut a length of yarn A and thread onto yarn needle, tying a knot on the other end. Pull in from the bottom of the head and up and out so that the yarn emerges where one of the ears should be. Tug gently to pull the knot inside the head, and it will catch and secure on the stuffing. Using your yarn needle, create a running stitch that wraps around one and a half of the stitches on the head. Continue wrapping the yarn around this one stitch eight times more, then fasten off. Repeat for other ear.

BODY

With A, cast on 3 sts.
Round 1: [Kfb] 3 times. Distribute sts evenly over 3 dpns and join to work in the round. (6 sts)
Round 2: [Kfb] 6 times (12 sts)
Round 3: [K1, kfb] 6 times. (18 sts)
Rounds 4–9: Knit.
Round 10: K9. Place last 9 sts of round on waste yarn.

FIRST LEG:

Distribute remaining 9 sts over 3 dpns and join to work in the round. Knit 5 rounds over these 9 sts. Cut yarn, thread yarn onto yarn needle, and thread through live sts, stuffing body and leg before pulling tight.

SECOND LEG:

Distribute 9 held sts over 3 dpns and join yarn. Complete as for First Leg.

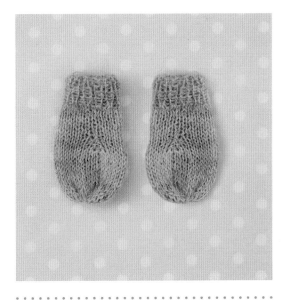

ARMS (make 2):

With A, cast on 6 sts.

Round 1: Knit. Distribute sts evenly over 3 dpns and join to work in the round.

Rounds 2–6: Knit.

Cut yarn, thread yarn onto yarn needle, thread through live sts and pull tight to tie off. Sew cast-on edge to body.

Finishing

Close any hole formed between legs. Weave in ends. Wash gently and lay flat to dry if desired.

Socks

You will need:

- Set of four US size 1 (2.25 mm) double-pointed knitting needles (dpns)
- Small amount of lace-weight yarn
- Yarn needle

Gauge

9.5 sts by 11 rows = 1 in (2.5 cm) square in stockinette stitch

INSTRUCTIONS

Cast on 24 sts, distribute evenly over 3 dpns and join to work in the round.

Rounds 1–10: [K1, p1] 12 times.

Rounds 11–18: Knit.

Round 19: K8, kfb, k6, kfb, k8. (26 sts)

Round 20: K9, kfb, k6, kfb, k9. (28 sts)

Round 21: K10, kfb, k6, kfb, k10. (30 sts)

Round 22: K11, kfb, k6, kfb, k11. (32 sts)

Rounds 23–30: Knit.

Round 31: [K2tog] 16 times. (16 sts)

Round 32: [K2tog] 8 times. (8 sts)

Cut yarn, thread yarn onto a yarn needle, leaving a long tail. Thread yarn through remaining sts, pull tight, and tie off. Repeat for other sock.

Finishing

Weave in ends. Wash gently and lay flat to dry if desired.

Superhero accessories

FRONT

You will need:

- Pair of US size 4 (3.5 mm) knitting needles
- 75 yd (70 m) of fingering-weight yarn
- US size E-4 (3.5 mm) crochet hook
- Waste yarn
- Yarn needle

Gauge
13 sts by 19 rows = 2 in (5 cm) in stockinette stitch

INSTRUCTIONS
MASK
Cast on 10 sts.
Rows 1–14: Knit.
Row 15: K1, bind off 8 sts (to leave 1 st rem after bind off on needle). (2 sts: 1 each side of bind off)
Row 16: K1, Cast on 8 sts, k1.
Starting with a RS row, work in st st for 10 rows.

TOP PART OF EYE HOLE:
Row 27 (RS): K1, kfb, k1, k2tog, turn.
Row 28: P2tog, p1, pfb, p1, turn.
Row 29: K3, k2tog, turn.
Rows 30, 32, and 34: Purl.
Row 31: K2tog, k1, kfb, turn.
Row 33: K3, kfb, turn.
Row 35: Knit. Leave these 5 sts on waste yarn (do not break yarn).

BOTTOM PART OF EYE HOLE:
With RS facing, join yarn to 5 sts remaining on needle.
Row 27 (RS): K2tog, k3.
Row 28: Purl.
Row 29: K2tog, k2.
Work in st st for 3 more rows. Break yarn.

BACK

JOIN TOP AND BOTTOM:
Row 1 (RS): Place 5 sts from top on RH needle, k3 across bottom sts. (8 sts)
Row 2: Purl.
Row 3: K2tog, k4, k2tog. (6 sts)
Row 4: Purl.
Row 5: K2tog, k2, k2tog. (4 sts)
Work in st st for 4 more rows.
Row 10 (RS): Kfb, k2, kfb. (6 sts)
Row 11: Purl.
Row 12: Kfb, k4, kfb. (8 sts)
Row 13: Purl.

TOP PART OF EYE HOLE:
Row 1 (RS): K5, turn.
Rows 2, 4, and 6: Purl.
Row 3: K3, k2tog.
Row 5: Kfb, k1, k2tog.
Row 7: K3, kfb.
Row 8 (WS): Pfb, p1, p2tog, p1.
Row 9: K2tog, k2, kfb. Leave these 5 sts on waste yarn (do not break yarn).

BOTTOM PART OF EYE HOLE:

With RS facing, join yarn to 3 sts remaining on needle. Work in st st for 3 rows.

Row 4 (WS): P2, pfb.

Row 5: Knit.

Row 6: P3, pfb.

JOIN TOP AND BOTTOM:

Next row (RS): Place 5 sts from top on RH needle, k5 across bottom sts. (10 sts)

Work 9 more rows in st st.

Row 11: K1, bind off 8 sts (to leave 1 st rem after bind off on needle). (2 sts: 1 each side of bind off)

Row 12: K1, cast on 8 sts, k1.

Rows 13–27: Knit.

Finishing

Attach yarn at top of mask between garter stitch section and first ear hole. With crochet hook, single crochet across top of mask to other ear hole. Fasten off. With crochet hook, work single crochet around each eye hole. Weave in ends. Wash gently and lay flat to dry if desired.

CAPE

Cast on 40 sts.

Rows 1–3: Knit

Row 4 (WS): K2, purl to last 2 sts, k2.

Row 5 (RS): Knit.

Rows 6–22: Repeat Rows 4–5 eight times more, then repeat Row 4 once more.

Row 23 (RS): K9, sk2p, k16, sk2p, k9. (36 sts)

Row 24: K2, purl to last 2 sts, k2.

Row 25: K8, sk2p, k14, sk2p, k8. (32 sts)

Row 26: K2, purl to last 2 sts, k2.

Row 27: K7, sk2p, k12, sk2p, k7. (28 sts)

Row 28: K2, purl to last 2 sts, k2.

Row 29: K6, sk2p, k10, sk2p, k6. (24 sts)

Rows 30–33: Work in st st.

Rows 34–37: Knit.

Bind off all sts.

Finishing

Weave in ends. Wash gently and lay flat to dry if desired. Cut a 12-in (30-cm) piece of yarn, thread onto yarn needle, and weave yarn through neck edge of cape (Row 37). Knot each end; use yarn to tie cape around bear's neck.

Pullover sweater

You will need:
- Set of five US size 5 (3.75 mm) double-pointed knitting needles (dpns)
- 60 yd (55 m) of worsted-weight yarn
- Small amount of worsted-weight yarn in contrasting color (optional)
- Waste yarn
- Yarn needle

Gauge

11 sts by 16 rows = 2 in (5 cm) square in stockinette stitch

Note

To work in a stripe pattern, work Rounds 6, 9, and 12 of Body and Sleeves and Round 15 of Yoke in a contrasting color; work all other rounds in main color.

INSTRUCTIONS

BODY:

Cast on 42 sts. Distribute sts evenly over 3 dpns and join to work in the round.

Rounds 1–2: [K1, p1] 21 times.

Rounds 3–12: Knit.

Place all sts on a piece of waste yarn and set aside.

SLEEVES:

Cast on 18 sts. Distribute sts evenly over 3 dpns and join to work in the round.

Rounds 1–2: [K1, p1] 9 times.

Rounds 3–12: Knit.

Place all sts on a piece of waste yarn and set aside. Repeat for other sleeve.

YOKE

Distribute sts (do not knit) as follows: on first dpn: first 11 sts of Body and first 9 sts of first Sleeve; on second dpn: next 9 sts of first Sleeve and next 10 sts of Body; on third dpn: next 10 sts of Body and first 9 sts of second Sleeve; and finally on fourth dpn: next 9 sts of second Sleeve and last 11 sts of Body. (78 sts)

Join yarn.

Round 1: K9, [k2tog] twice, k14, [k2tog] twice, k16, [k2tog] twice, k14, [k2tog] twice, k9. Join to work in the round. (70 sts)

Round 2: K8, [k2tog] twice, k12, [k2tog] twice, k14, [k2tog] twice, k12, [k2tog] twice, k8. (62 sts)

Round 3: K7, [k2tog] twice, k10, [k2tog] twice, k12, [k2tog] twice, k10, [k2tog] twice, k7. (54 sts)

Round 4: [K2tog] 27 times. (27 sts)

Rounds 5–7: [K1, p1] 13 times, k1.

Bind off all sts.

Finishing

Weave in ends. Wash gently and lay flat to dry if desired.

Elf hat

You will need:

- Set of five US size 5 (3.75 mm) double-pointed knitting needles (dpns)
- 20 yd (18 m) of worsted-weight yarn in green (color A)
- 20 yd (18 m) of worsted-weight yarn in natural (color B)
- Yarn needle

Gauge
11 sts by 16 rows = 2 in (5 cm) square in stockinette stitch

Note
STRIPE PATTERN
Round 1: Work in A.
Round 2: Work in B.
Rep last 2 rounds for pattern.

INSTRUCTIONS
With A, cast on 48 sts.
Round 1: [K1, p1] 24 times. Distribute sts evenly over 4 dpns and join to work in the round.
Rounds 2–5: [K1, p1] around.
Join B and continue in Stripe Pattern for remainder of hat.
Rounds 6–7: Knit.
Round 8: K10, bind off 6 sts, k18 (for 19 sts on needle after last bind off), bind off 6 sts, knit to end of round.
Round 9: K10, cast on 6 sts, k19, cast on 6 sts, knit to end of round.
Rounds 10–11: Knit. Redistribute sts if necessary to make sure there are 12 sts on each dpn.
Begin decreases:

Round 12: [Knit to 2 sts before end of needle, k2tog] 4 times. (4 sts decreased)
Rounds 13–15: Knit.
Round 16: Repeat Round 12.
Round 17: Knit.
Rep Rounds 16–17 six times more. (16 sts)
Round 30: Repeat Round 12. (12 sts)
Rounds 31–33: Knit.
Round 34: Repeat Round 12. (8 sts)
Rounds 35–37: Knit.
Round 38: [K2tog] 4 times. (4 sts)
Rounds 39–42: Knit.
Cut both yarns, thread onto a yarn needle together, and pull through remaining stitches. Tie off.

Finishing
Weave in ends. Wash gently and lay flat to dry if desired.

Bear necessities

Tools and materials

The right tools and materials will make your knitting project much more straightforward and enjoyable. Small toys are a great project, because you can use the materials you already have on hand. However, here are our suggestions for tools and materials you might want to gather before starting your project.

Yarn (various types) (1)
Each project lists the suggested yarn to use. Yarn comes in many different thicknesses (or "weights") and fiber types. Most of the projects in this book use wool yarn because of its versatility and durability. Of course, you can use any fiber type to make a stuffed bear. Your finished project will vary based on what you use, and that's part of the fun of it.

Knitting needles (various sizes) (2)
The needle size used for each of the projects in this book is mentioned alongside the pattern. Sometimes double-pointed needles are used, which come in a set of four or five and have points on both ends. Regular knitting needles are also used, and they come in a set of two and have points on only one end. Needles are available in a number

of different materials, including metal, wood, and plastic. Try them all out to find which type is most comfortable for you.

Scissors (3 and 11)
It's always handy to have a nice small pair of sharp scissors during a knitting project. You'll need them for snipping off yarn ends and surplus threads.

Polyester fiberfill (4)
Fiberfill is a type of stuffing made from polyester fibers. It holds its shape fairly well, and keeps your stuffed toy fluffy and full for a long time.

Safety eyes (5)
These eyes are available in many sizes and colors. The patterns that use them specify which size

you will need in millimeters. You can buy safety eyes with plastic or metal washer backings.

Buttons (6)
Button eyes give a classic look to any stuffed bear. They are available in every size and color imaginable. They are also used when making a jointed bear.

Crochet hook (7)
All of the projects in this book are knitted, but a few accessories are finished off with a crochet hook. These also come in a wide variety of sizes and materials, but the most useful one for the projects detailed here will be a size E.

Stitch markers (8)

Stitch markers are little plastic or metal rings that sit between two stitches on your knitting. These can simplify patterns by holding your place between two stitches and letting you know when to repeat a certain action, like a decrease.

Embroidery floss (9)

Embroidery floss is usually made from cotton or rayon and is available in many colors. It is used to embroider the faces onto the bears, so you will need black or very dark brown for this.

Yarn needle (10)

A yarn needle is short, thick, and blunt. The eye is large enough to accommodate even the thickest of yarns, and the tip is not sharp, so it won't split your stitches while seaming your projects together.

Embroidery needle (12)

These come in a wide variety of sizes. You only need one that has an eye large enough to thread through embroidery floss, but it also needs to be thin and with a point so that you can split your stitches while embroidering something like a bear's smile.

Small ruler and/or measuring tape (13)

You will want to check and make sure your work is the size it needs to be, or check your gauge. A small measuring tape or ruler will get the job done!

Wool roving (14)

This material consists of a long bundle of loose wool fibers. It's a good natural alternative to fiberfill and also comes in many colors. This makes it useful for toys that have a loose gauge, as you can pick a shade that matches your yarn color so that it won't be as visible behind the stitches.

Stitch holders (not pictured)

Stitch holders look like large metal safety pins, and they are used to hold active stitches while you work on a different part of the piece. You can use a standard stitch holder, or an extra double-pointed needle, or even a piece of waste yarn threaded through your stitches with a yarn needle.

What is gauge?

Gauge is the size of a knitting stitch knitted on a specific needle using a specific technique. If your stitches are larger, your fabric will be looser, and if your stitches are smaller, your fabric will be tighter. Since everyone's knitting is going to end up being slightly different, we use gauge to measure whether our finished item will be the same size as the one knitted by the designer. While this is very important for knitting projects like sweaters and socks that need to have a good fit, it's not quite as important for stuffed toys. For the stuffed bears in this book, you mainly want to be sure that your gauge is tight enough so that you aren't going to have stuffing poking through your stitches. It is a little more important for the accessories for the bears, as you want things to fit properly. If your bear turned out a little larger than expected, you might want to go up a needle size or two for the accessories to accompany it, and vice versa for a smaller bear.

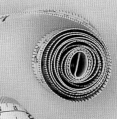

Making faces

When you're making a stuffed toy, the face is probably the most important part. A perfectly knitted bear is nothing without a cute face to give it personality and warmth. When you're adding a face to your toy, you have to really experiment and decide what you like the best. You can use the pattern pictures as a guide, but you also want to take a good look at your knitting and find the best place to put the features.

Positioning safety eyes

When using safety eyes, you can do a little test by putting the eyes in but not fastening the backs, and checking to see if they look right.

Eyes tight to center
In this position, the eyes are very close to the nose, and positioned just slightly above it. This gives the bear a sort of babyish look, as the close-together features emphasize the oversized head.

Eyes slightly higher and farther apart
The eyes are a bit higher and a few stitches farther from the nose. This is the classic teddy bear look and a great place to start when you are trying to decide where to place the eyes. It looks good on just about all teddy-bear shapes and sizes.

Eyes farthest apart
The eyes are almost halfway back to the ears and only slightly higher than the nose. This position can give your bear a vintage look, but it can be difficult to make sure the eyes are even at such a distance. Be sure to check from several angles before you secure the backs of the safety eyes.

Attaching safety eyes

Acrylic safety eyes come in two pieces: a black eye with a post backing and a plastic washer. When the washer is pushed down over the post, it is permanently affixed.

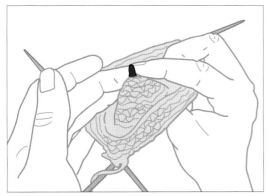

1. Visualize where on your bear's face you would like to attach the pair of safety eyes.

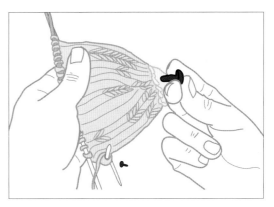

2. Push the first eye through the fabric.

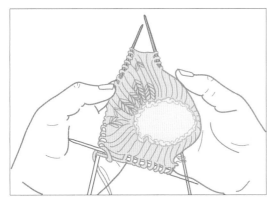

3. Push the second eye through the fabric and make sure the two eyes are level. Check that the post of each eye goes cleanly through the knitted fabric without splitting any stitches.

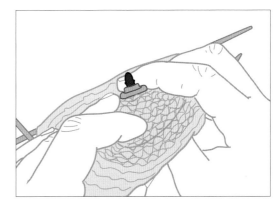

4. Push each backing down on the post of each eye, ensuring that it clicks into place.

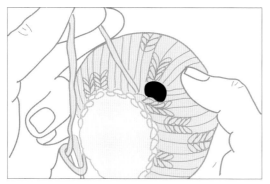

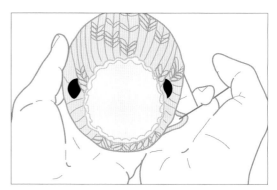

Structuring the face

When your bear head is fully assembled and has the eyes in place, you may want to add more depth by using a few stitches to pull in the eyes a little bit. This gives your bear a bit of subtle shaping that knitting stitches alone are unable to achieve.

1. Cut a length of yarn the same color as your bear's head. Thread it onto a yarn needle. Attach this yarn with a knot underneath the head where it will be sewn to the body. Insert the yarn needle into the head and pull it out just in front of one of the eyes. Don't pull it too tightly—you don't want to create a dimple in the bottom of the head.

Embroidering faces

As with the eyes, you may want to experiment a little before adding your nose and mouth. Try laying a small piece of your embroidery floss on the face in the configuration that your mouth will be, and really inspect your stitches to see where you can anchor your nose and mouth. Use embroidery floss and an embroidery needle to do this. Work the nose and mouth in short, interlocking stitches. Don't be afraid to rip them out and start over if you don't like how it turned out. After all, it's one of the most important parts of your bear!

Triangle nose and upside-down "V" mouth

Rectangle nose and small smile

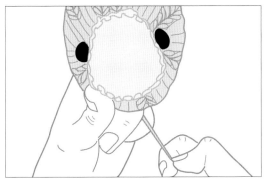

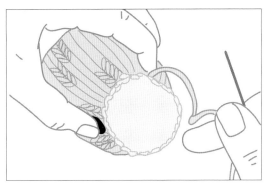

2. Hold the bear head between your thumb and index finger. Squeeze the two eyes together slightly—you will be able to see the way that it changes the shape of the bear's face. When you are happy with the shape, take the yarn needle in your other hand and put it back into the bear's head, a stitch away from where it originally came out. Pull the needle back out in front of the other eye, just tight enough so that the yarn is taut between your squeezing fingers.

3. Repeat the process, going back and forth between the eyes three or four times, placing your stitches all the way around the eyes. When you let go of the head, the face should still be pulled in around the eyes. To finish, push the needle back in near one of the eyes, but this time pull it down through the head to the original place where you attached it. Tie off the yarn, and pull any loose ends inside the head. If you have visible knots, they will be covered when you sew the head to the body.

Horizontally stitched nose and wide smile

Vertically stitched nose and uneven grin

Long vertical line between nose and mouth

Short vertical line between nose and mouth

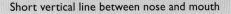

Assembling your bear

In almost all of the patterns in this book, the bear's head, body, and limbs are all knitted separately and then sewn together. You can use the yarn that you knitted the bear with to sew him or her together, unless you used a very furry or highly textured yarn. If that is the case, it may not be strong enough to use, and you should use a similar-colored, plain yarn.

Stuffing and shaping

Stuffing your projects is a simple task but will vary slightly from pattern to pattern. You will usually want to stuff as you go, to some extent.

Head

Start with a small bit of fiberfill and stuff it into the tip of the nose. Pull off another, slightly larger piece, and stuff it behind the first. Continue in this fashion until you feel the muzzle is adequately stuffed. Next, pull a larger ball of stuffing and work it into the head. Be sure that the stuffing in the muzzle does not become displaced, or your bear's face will become flat. Push the stuffing around with your fingers as necessary before closing up the last opening on the head (see "Finishing techniques," page 107).

Body

Stuffing the body is very simple. If your body has any shaping (like a potbelly), first put smaller bits of fiber to stuff the part that sticks out the most, then fill in with larger bunches of fiber. You usually want the body to be stuffed firmly, but do not put so much in there that it stretches your stitches out.

To ensure that your bear is evenly stuffed begin with smaller bits of fiberfill and build up as necessary. Be aware that some areas may need specific shaping, such as a potbelly.

Limbs

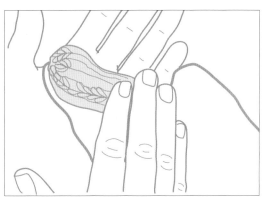

1. Push a small bit of fiber down to the very end of the limb into the hand or foot. Continue using similar-sized pieces of fiber and push them in behind the first one, being careful not to push too hard.

2. Once the entire limb is stuffed, roll it between your hands to remove any lumps. If your bear's feet are too spherical, you will need to sew a few stitches in them to flatten them out.

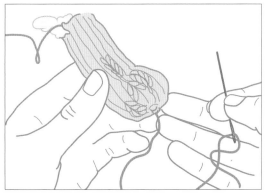

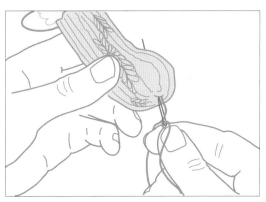

3. Attach a length of yarn to the bottom of the foot with a knot through a stitch. Thread the yarn onto a yarn needle. Stick the needle directly into the bottom of the foot. You want it to emerge out of the top of the foot, just in front of where it meets the leg. Pull slightly, but not too hard.

4. Stick the needle back into the foot, slightly in front of where your yarn came out. Push it through the foot again, coming out near where you attached the yarn. Pull slightly again, and the foot should start to flatten out. Sew a few more stitches in this way until you get the shape you want. Tie off and pull any loose ends inside the foot.

Attaching limbs and head onto the body

Once you've knitted your bear's head, body, and limbs separately, you'll need to sew them together. Mattress stitch is a good choice for sewing up seams (see page 105.) Seaming the different body parts is straightforward and the process is largely the same regardless of the limb you are working on. Usually, the first elements you sew together are the head and the body. You will need a length of yarn and a yarn needle.

1. Attach the yarn to the body and tie it on with a simple knot. Thread the yarn onto a yarn needle.

2. Hold the head and body together in your hand, squishing them together slightly so that there is a flat surface created between the two pieces.

3. Slip the yarn needle through one stitch of the head, around the "flat surface" where the two pieces are pushed together.

4. Slip the yarn needle through one stitch of the body, below your last stitch.

5. Keep going around the flat surface where the two pieces are pushed together, putting one stitch in the head, then one stitch in the body. When you get halfway around the head, pull the yarn tight.

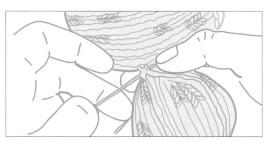

6. Continue taking one stitch of the head and one stitch of the body, until you get back to where you started. Pull the yarn tight again. Tie off, pulling any loose ends into the body.

Making a jointed bear

While only one pattern in this book is depicted with button joints, you could make almost any bear you desired a jointed bear. These steps outline how to create moveable joints on your bear's limbs. Note: do not give a bear with button joints to a baby, as the buttons could become loose and be a choking hazard.

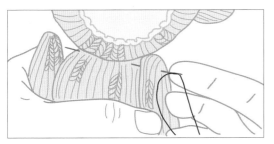

1. Gather together a long sewing needle, four buttons, and a strong thread—such as an upholstery or button thread. Cut a length of thread and thread it onto the needle. Tie a knot in the other end. Starting with the arms, position them on the sides of the body. Hold the three pieces sandwiched together in one hand. With the other hand, stick the needle through one arm, all the way through the body, and out the other arm. Don't pull too hard—you don't want your knot to pull through the stuffing.

2. Push the needle back into the arm, very close (but not exactly in the same spot) to where you pulled it out. Again, push it all the way through the body and out the other arm. Repeat this a few times, keeping the threads running through the body all parallel and very close together.

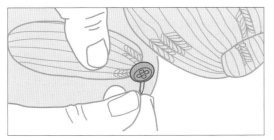

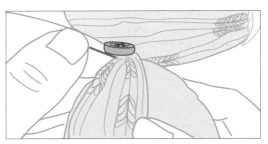

3. After just a few stitches the arms should feel secure but still move freely. At this point, sew the buttons over the joints on each side by holding a button in front of where you will pull the needle out, and pulling the needle out through one of the holes. Insert the needle back in the opposite hole on the button. Repeat on the other arm. Repeat this a few more times until your buttons are secure.

4. Insert the needle through the button, and through the body as if to do another stitch all the way through, but instead of pulling it out through the hole of the next button, pull it out under the next button. Knot off your thread by wrapping the thread around the needle twice and pulling tight. Cut the thread, concealing the knot beneath the button. Repeat these steps for the legs.

Core techniques

Slip-knot cast on (CO)
Putting a slip knot on the needle makes your first stitch. You can coil the yarn around your fingers or lay it flat.

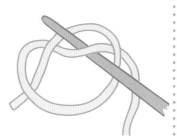

1. Coil the yarn into a loop, then bring the strand forward and through the loop. Insert the needle as shown to secure the yarn.

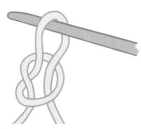

2. Pull one end to tighten the knot, then gently pull the other end of the yarn to close the knot up to the needle. You are now ready to cast on.

Knit cast on (KCO)
Insert the right needle into the first stitch on the left needle as if to knit, and pull a loop forward. Place the loop back onto the left needle. This loop is now your first stitch. Repeat.

Knit stitch
Hold the yarn and needles in whichever way feels most comfortable to you.

1. Insert the right needle into the first stitch on the left needle. Make sure that it goes from left to right into the front of the stitch.

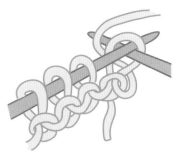

2. Taking the yarn behind, bring it up and around the right needle.

3. Using the tip of the right needle, draw a loop of yarn through the stitch.

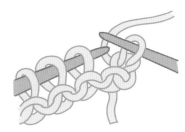

4. Slip the stitch off the left needle. There is now a new stitch on the right needle.

Garter stitch

Knitting every stitch of every row produces a stitch pattern known as garter stitch. Garter stitch makes an elastic fabric in which the stitches are stretched widthwise, while the rows draw up to give an almost-square gauge.

Purl stitch

Hold the yarn and needles in the same way as for making a knit stitch.

1. Insert the right needle into the first stitch on the left needle. Make sure that it goes into the front of the stitch from right to left.

2. Taking the yarn to the front, loop it around the right needle.

3. Lower the tip of the right needle, taking it away from you to draw a loop of yarn through the stitch.

4. Slip the stitch off the left needle. There is now a new stitch on the right needle.

Stockinette stitch

The best-known combination of knit and purl is called stockinette stitch. It is very simple—just knit one row and purl one row alternately.

Mattress stitch on stockinette stitch

Place the pieces with the right sides facing. Thread a blunt-ended needle with yarn. Insert the needle under the horizontal bar between the first two stitches on one side. Then insert the needle under the bar between the same stitches on the opposite side. Draw the yarn through. Repeat for each stitch.

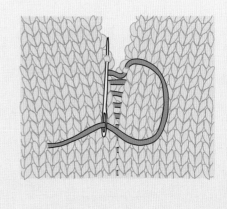

Knit front back (Kfb)

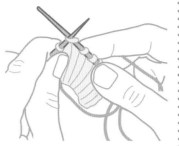

1. Knit through the front loop of the next stitch, but do not slip the stitch off the left needle.

2. Then knit through the back loop of the same stitch and slip the stitch off the left needle.

3. You will have increased by one stitch.

Knit two together (K2tog)

Knitting two stitches together on a knit row makes a smooth shaping, with the second stitch lying on top of the first.

1. Insert the right needle through the front of the first two stitches on the left needle, then take the yarn around the needle.

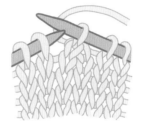

2. Draw the loop through and drop the two stitches off the left needle.

Purl two together (P2tog)

For a decrease worked on a purl row that slants to the right on the knit side of the fabric, purl two stitches together.

Make one (M1)

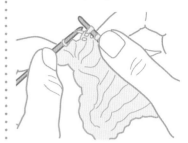

1. Make one stitch by inserting the needle into the bar before the next stitch and pulling up a loop.

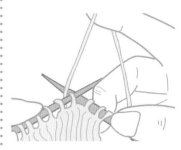

2. Knit into the back of the strand on the left-hand needle. You will have increased by one stitch.

Double decrease

Slip one, knit two together, pass slipped stitch over (Sl1, k2tog, psso).
Slip one stitch, knit the next two stitches together, then pass the slipped stitch over the stitch resulting from the k2tog. You will have decreased by two stitches.

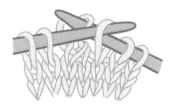

Finishing techniques

When you are done knitting each piece of your bear, you will have to tie off the yarn and hide the ends. You want to be sure that your knots are tight and secure, so that your bear doesn't fall apart during regular play. With a bit of practice, you will find the best technique for your work and tying off and weaving in ends will be quick and easy.

Weaving in ends

When working with a stuffed item, it is very simple to weave in ends. Thread any offending end onto the yarn needle, and pull it into the stuffed item. Pull it back out through the other side, and clip it off with scissors where it comes through the knit fabric.

Tying off

When you are finished knitting a piece of your project, you will need to tie off the yarn. Many of the projects in this book, end with "thread yarn through remaining live stitches, pull tight, and tie off."

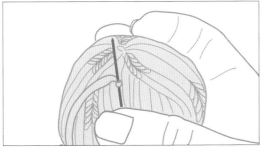

1. To "tie off," you should start by pushing your yarn needle through the tiny circle and then pull the yarn until it is tight. You want the needle to come back out of the piece a few stitches below the circle. Give it a little tug to make sure that the circle is still as tight as it can be.

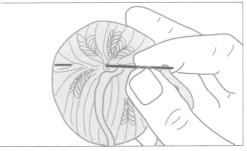

2. If you look closely at the stitches where your needle just came out, and pull them apart slightly, you will see a little bar of yarn between them. Push the tip of the yarn needle under this bar, but do not pull it through yet.

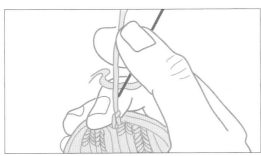

3. Wrap the yarn around the tip of the yarn needle twice. Pull the yarn needle all the way through, and give it a tug. The wraps you just did will form a knot.

4. Push the yarn needle back in, just above the knot, and pull back out somewhere else on the piece. This will pull the knot inside the fabric. Cut the yarn at the surface of the fabric.

Abbreviations

[],(), *	Work instructions in brackets/parentheses/after asterisk as many times as designated
cm	centimeter(s)
foll	follow(ing)
k	knit
k2tog	Knit the next two stitches together (1 stitch decreased)
kfb	Knit through both the front and back loops of a single stitch (1 stitch increased)
Kfbf	Knit through the front, then the back, then the front loop again of a single stitch (2 stitches increased)
in	inch(es)
LH	left-hand
m	meter(s)
M1	Pick up bar between stitches using left-hand needle from back to front; knit into bar (1 stitch increased)
mm	millimeter(s)
p	purl
pfb	Purl through both the front and back loops of a single stitch (1 stitch increased)
p2tog	purl two stitches together (1 stitch decreased)
pm	place marker
psso	pass slipped stitch over
rem	remain(ing)
rep	repeat(s)
RH	right-hand
RS	right side
sk2p	Slip 1 stitch, knit the next two stitches together, pass slipped stitch over (2 stitches decreased)
sl	slip stitch
ssk	slip 2 stitches separately knit-wise, slip stitches back to left-hand needle, and knit 2 stitches together through back of loops
st st	Stockinette stitch (knit all RS rows and purl all WS rows)
st(s)	stitch(es)
w&t	(wrap and turn) On RS, slip 1 stitch purl-wise, bring yarn to front, slip 1 stitch back to left-hand needle, bring yarn to back, turn. On WS, slip 1 stitch purl-wise, bring yarn to back, slip 1 stitch back to left-hand needle, bring yarn to front, turn.
WS	wrong side
wyib	with yarn in back
wyif	with yarn in front
yd	yard(s)

Index

Credits

Publisher acknowledgments:
All step-by-step and other images are the copyright of Quarto Publishing plc. While every effort has been made to credit contributors, Quarto would like to apologize should there have been any omissions or errors—and would be pleased to make the appropriate correction for future editions of the book.

Author acknowledgments:
Special thanks to Mark Carroll and Regina Small for offering constant support and encouragement over the many years that I've been doing knitting work; and to Jude and Ivy Carroll, for providing an endless world of imagination and inspiration in my daily life.

With special thanks to Cascade Yarns for providing the yarns used in this book.
www.cascadeyarns.com